# BOY SCOUTS

BY
"GILCRAFT"

London
C. Arthur Pearson Ltd.
Henrietta Street

*First published* 1930

Printed in Great Britain at
*The Mayflower Press, Plymouth.*   William Brendon & Son, Ltd.

# FOREWORD

AFTER the glorious adventure of Brownsea Island and the thrills of starting a Troop whilst *Scouting for Boys* was still coming out in parts, I realised quite painfully how little I knew and how much I must depend upon the experience of others.

*Scouting for Boys* did then, and must always, supply the foundation of Scouting, a foundation upon which we Scoutmasters must build if we would run a successful Troop, and *Scouting for Boys* must always be our main inspiration and guide, but we are glad to have the help and advice of brother Scouters, and to profit by their failures and successes.

Mistakes we shall always make, and it will be a sad day for the Movement when we have no opportunity of making mistakes. But the more we can limit them the better.

I am sure, therefore, that the whole Movement will welcome Gilcraft's book, because it supplies splendid materials for building upon the foundations given in *Scouting for Boys*, and with Gilcraft to help us, it would really seem almost impossible to go astray !

He has accumulated the wisdom of twenty-one years' Scouting —read, heard, seen and practised. He has digested it and brought it forth as a comprehensive, easily understood handbook.

I offer just three pieces of advice :

(1) Read it in conjunction with—not in place of—*Scouting for Boys*.

(2) Take it in small doses, or you may suffer from mental indigestion.

(3) Interpret it all in terms of the boys in your care.

P. W. EVERETT,
*Chief Scout's Commissioner.*

# CONTENTS

7

8 CONTENTS

# BOY SCOUTS

## CHAPTER I

### THE ARCHITECT'S TRAINING

SCOUTING, having come of age, is accepted by many people without thought and without enquiry ; but every worker in the Movement should have some knowledge as to how it began. Its meanings and its aims cannot be properly understood until its origin is known, and its origin is obviously intimately connected with its Founder —the Architect of the whole fabric of Scouting.

Every Scouter and would-be Scouter, that is, every man and woman who is a worker in Scouting, or who is attracted to it, should have sufficient knowledge of its beginnings to justify his or her connection with a Movement which some say is militarist, some pacificist, which some say is for rich boys only, some for the more unfortunate boys who live in poor homes amongst squalid surroundings. Each one should be prepared to meet the criticisms which he or she is bound to encounter at unexpected moments and in unexpected places.

### How Scouting Began

In order to answer the question, How and when did the Boy Scout Movement start ? we have to go back to its Founder's own boyhood, for the idea of Scouting for Boys was in Robert Baden-Powell's mind long before he made the scheme public, long before he made any experiments as a soldier in the training of men.

In his early years, he and his four brothers had a small sailing yacht, manned by themselves, in which they had many exciting adventures, and in which they learnt, by actual experience, how to be useful and self-reliant. The future Chief Scout learned how to cook ; he came to understand all about rowing and the management of boats ; he learned how to swim ; how to tie knots ; how to build shelters ; and—what is even more important—how to have a thoroughly good time in healthy, natural surroundings.

In his boyhood, Baden-Powell also went on tramping expeditions. He explored parts of his own country, sleeping out of doors, studying animals, birds and plants, sketching, finding his way by the stars, going over factories, learning how things were made, and

9

generally picking up—and remembering—all the information about all sorts of things that he possibly could.

This was the beginning of Scouting for Boys as applied to the Chief Scout's own boyhood, and these early experiences which he found so attractive, and at the same time so useful to himself and his brothers, later on gave him the inspiration for his successful methods of training the young soldiers in his care.

While working with his regiment in India in 1893 Robert Baden-Powell realised that the training his men were given was not sufficient to fit them for their duties as cavalry. Gradually he introduced practices which trained them to be self-reliant, to be able to find their way through the country on their own, to take care of themselves and their horses. The results of this training were eventually published in a little book entitled *Aids to Scouting*. This book dealt with such subjects as—the Importance of the Scout ; Pluck, Self-reliance and Discretion ; Finding Your Way in a Strange Country ; Quickness of Eye ; Keeping Yourself Hidden ; Tracking ; Reporting ; Scouting ; and so on.

These lectures, originally written for the 5th Dragoon Guards, attracted considerable attention in the Army, but no one could have conceived that they heralded the birth of a great army of Peace.

As is well known, when Baden-Powell with his small force was surrounded in Mafeking during the Boer War, he was compelled to use the boys of Mafeking as messengers, orderlies and lookouts. The organisation of this corps was the work of Lord Edward Cecil, but the response of the boys to the training they received made a great impression on the Commander of the garrison.

So it is, possibly, that it was in Mafeking in time of war that the future Founder of Scouting for Boys first came consciously to realise what an instrument for the training of boys was lying to his hand in the past training he had given the men of the 5th Dragoon Guards.

When the Boer War was over, Baden-Powell was entrusted with the raising and organising of the South African Constabulary, the force which gradually took over the responsibility for the peace and good order of the country from the British Army. Here again he put the same kind of training into practice, but in a more complete form. Gradually he had come to realise that the Army could never be treated just as a machine, that each member of it ought to be turned into a self-reliant, thinking unit. So in the Constabulary he appealed to the human side of his men ; he trusted them on their honour to do certain things ; he organised them into Patrols of six with a Leader over each Patrol ; he dressed them in a uniform very like that of the now familiar Boy Scout uniform.

On returning to England in 1903 Baden-Powell found that his exploits in Mafeking had fired the imagination of a number of people, and had, in consequence, drawn attention to some of the methods he had employed in the past in his training of men to be war Scouts. He found that various training classes for teachers were using *Aids to Scouting* as a text-book in order to secure training in observation and deduction. Very definitely the successive stages of his experiments had been linked together, and pointed the way to the training of boys, not for military reasons, but for peace work in their own homes, in their own country.

The way pointed out to him seemed clear, and in 1905, after consultation with the leaders of certain boy movements, he offered to write a book which would contain a programme of training that could be used by the then existing organisations for boys, such as the Y.M.C.A., Boys' Brigade, Church Lads' Brigade, Cadets, and others.

In order to try out his ideas in actual practice an experimental camp was held at Brownsea Island in Poole Harbour in August, 1907. The camp was conducted as a Troop of Scouts divided into four Patrols. The boys were drawn from different classes and from different localities. They were given a week's instruction in Scouting, and " though the boys got but a mere smattering of the proposed teaching, its methods and scope were put to a good practical test."

This camp and its results confirmed his plan of work and encouraged Baden-Powell to go ahead with the writing of the book. He gathered together books on work among boys, on methods used in Ireland, in England, in Japan, in Zululand ; he studied the customs of the Knights of the Round Table, the books of Seton Thompson, of Dan Beard. He was determined that the success of his scheme was not to be endangered by lack of preparation.

In November, 1907, three leaflets were published and distributed. The first of these, entitled *A Suggestion*, and actually written the previous May, set out various reasons for the introduction of Scouting ; the second gave *A Summary of the Scheme* suggested ; the third, headed *A Successful Trial*, gave an account of the camp at Brownsea Island. It is worthy of note that the first pamphlet mentioned that " a somewhat similar idea was started in America a short time back by Mr. Ernest Seton Thompson, and had already attained phenomenal success."

Early in 1908 *Scouting for Boys* was published in six fortnightly parts, and Scouting as we know it to-day was born. It was not all the plain sailing that people to-day imagine. We have forgotten to-day that Scouting was derided and impeached from the platform and the pulpit, and held up to ridicule in the Press.

Scouting came through its trials of infancy a healthy child, and in two years had a membership of 124,000 boys. What was intended as a programme to be used by other organisations had become a Movement which was attracting world-wide attention. The

Chief Scout, after seeking the advice of the highest man in the land, resigned his Army commission and resolved to give the rest of his life to the Movement he had founded. In 1912 a Royal Charter was granted to the Boy Scouts Association ; this grant can be regarded as marking the definite approval of the King and Government of a Movement which had shown that it could apply its aims and ideals in actual practice.

That briefly is how Scouting began ; but, as Lurgan Sahib explained to Kim, " since ' hows ' matter little in this world," we should try and understand " the ' why ' of everything."

The whole object of the Chief Scout's suggestion in 1907 was the development of good citizenship in Great Britain. His first pamphlet was headed by a quotation : " The same causes which brought about the downfall of the Great Roman Empire are working to-day in Great Britain." These causes were " the decline of good citizenship among its subjects, due to want of energetic patriotism, to the growth of luxury and idleness, and to the exaggerated importance of local party politics."

" I think," wrote Baden-Powell, " that we are only near to the parting of the ways where it becomes incumbent on every one of us who has the slightest patriotism in him earnestly to help, in however small a way, to turn the rising generation on to the right road for good citizenship."

To this end he offered his scheme of Scouting " as a possible aid towards putting on a positive footing the development, moral and physical, of boys of all creeds and classes, by a means which should appeal to them while offending as little as possible the susceptibilities of their elders."

As the years pass attitudes and values change, but the main " why " of Scouting remains the same—Good Citizenship. So it is that what was avowedly, and rightly, a patriotic movement initiated in Great Britain has spread throughout the world into almost every civilised country where the value of citizenship is appreciated.

In these modern days it is frequently the custom to decry patriotism as if it were a crime, and the source of all evil ; whereas, as every right-thinking man and woman knows, it is both the source and the outcome of co-operative effort. On more than one occasion Scouting has demonstrated the truth of the saying that internationalism is founded on nationalism, that they who would be the friends of all the world—like Kim—must first of all be the friends of their own neighbours.

Since the foundations of Scouting have been well and truly laid at home, its influence has spread beyond the bounds of any man's imaginings in 1907.

BOOKS.

*Aids to Scouting*, Baden-Powell. Gale and Polden, 1s.
*Twenty-One Years of Scouting*, Wade. Pearson, 7s. 6d.

## CHAPTER II

### THE ARCHITECT'S DESIGNS

" *Nations have passed away and left no traces,*
*And History gives the naked cause of it—*
*One single, simple reason in all cases ;*
*They fell because their peoples were not fit.*

. . . .

*The even heart that seldom slurs its beat—*
  *The cool head weighing what that heart desires—*
*The measuring eye that guides the hand and feet—*
  *The Soul unbroken when the body tires—*
*These are the things our weary world requires*
*Far more than superfluities of wit ;*
  *Wherefore we pray you, sons of generous sires,*
*Be fit—be fit ! For Honour's sake be fit."*
        (From the Preface to Rudyard Kipling's
        *Land and Sea Tales for Scouts and Guides.*)

THE Chief Scout says : " The term Scouting has come to mean a system of training in citizenship, through games, for boys and girls." We have already seen that Scouting's main objective is the development of good citizenship. Time and again has this point been emphasised. In *Aids to Scoutmastership*, which was first published in 1920, the Chief Scout answered the question, What is Scouting ? by defining it as " a game in which elder brothers (or sisters) can give their younger brothers healthy environment and encourage them to healthy activities such as will help them to develop citizenship."

In the building work that we set out to do we are helped by having before us the designs and plans that the Architect of Scouting has drawn out. Let us study them carefully and come to an understanding of them.

The first aim of Scouting is to develop a boy's personal character and initiative, and by this is meant that the boy is instilled with personal initiative, self-control, self-reliance, with a sense of honour, duty, service, responsibility, and is trained in the faculties of observation and deduction. These qualities form the basis on which a proper manhood can be built, a manhood which by reason of its foundation and training in handicrafts and good turns will merge into the useful citizen.

Scouting provides the wherewithal to produce the healthy citizen by the practice of healthy activities, such as Scouting games, camping, hiking, by the study of nature lore, physical fitness and cleanliness, and by its strong moral code.

Happiness is often largely the complement of physical and moral fitness, but Scouting again makes special provision for the exercise of this virtue by its adaptation of natural tendencies, such as the gang spirit, and by insisting on the fact that Scouters, the grown-ups who are privileged to be allowed to work with the boys, are team leaders, thus establishing a close relationship—elder brother-hood—as between man and boy. An appreciation of the wonders and beauties of nature leads also to the foundation of a normally cheerful and contented disposition.

Scouting aims at reaching its ideal of happy, healthy, helpful citizens through character training, handicrafts, health-training, brotherliness, and, we must add, religion.

Scouting does provide for character training by its insistence on the study of each individual boy, which is only possible when Scout Troops are kept within definite limits as regards numbers, by means of Scout practices, by a proper use of the Patrol System, by em-phasising the responsibility of the Patrol Leaders, and by the ob-servance of the Scout Law.

Badges encourage the study of handicrafts, and emphasise the importance of helpfulness. The badges which qualify a First-class Scout for the King's Scout are all service badges.

Health-training is provided for by exercises, games, singing, en-couragement of activities and life in the open air, and by introduc-tion to a knowledge of hygiene and the laws of health.

It is not necessary to dwell on the brotherliness of Scouting ; it is provided for by the Scout Law and by the relationship which the Chief Scout insists should exist between Scouter and Scout, between Scouter and Scouter and between Scout and Scout. Brotherliness is one of the attributes which formerly at any rate differentiated the Scout Movement from other organisations for boys.

Our belief is that the Scout Brotherhood is one which will offer very material help in leading peoples and countries to a realisation of their duties towards each other, and we are confirmed in this belief by the fact that the general public has of late been so greatly impressed by the value of the Movement not only to the individual boy but also to the world at large. Time and time again has it been proved that differences between men can be removed by the simple application of the Scout Law and Promise ; such differences do not normally arise as between boy and boy where simplicity and trust still hold sway.

It is necessary, however, to make mention of the importance of religion in Scouting, as this factor is frequently overlooked, or deliberately ignored or denied. Further consideration will be given to the subject later, but here we may ponder over the words that the Chief Scout spoke at the Manchester Conference in 1914 : " I think the basis of almost any religion is founded on reverence and one's duty to one's God and one's neighbour, and that at least is what we can teach—the practical line of what is best in every religion—by teaching reverence for God, reverence for others and reverence for themselves amongst the boys. Then there are the ' good turns ' to other people, whether small or great, and the

missioner's work and life saving. These things are what every
religion would gladly accept as their practical side."

It is not sufficient, however, for Scouting to make the boy into
a happy, healthy, helpful citizen ; it has, as the Chief has expressed
it, to harness him to work for the community, to fit him into his
own particular niche.

What is meant is that in his future work a Scout is not to be a
lone Scout, or to work with a lone Patrol or in a lone Troop. He
is to be fitted to take his place amongst his fellow-men so that he
can work together with them for the good of their communal social
life. Scouting hopes to achieve this end by its education in citizenship and by acting up to its watchword of helpfulness. There is
a very important point here which it would be well to emphasise.
Scouting does not mean to train boys to regard themselves in any
way apart from others, or to make them dissatisfied with life as it
is. Sometimes, when the personal element in its machinery is
weak, it would appear to have this tendency. We must be absolutely firm in our own minds that each boy is to be encouraged
to take his proper place in life, to make good there so that he
cannot be a burden on others or on the State, to consolidate his
own position, and not imperil it by adventitious essays in so-
called Knight Errantry. His first service to himself and others is
to establish himself. We must be firm too in our conception of
Scouting as embracing the whole of life, and not as something
apart from the lives of ordinary men and women. Our boys must
be trained so that they can mix with others as well as with each
other. That is one of the very important reasons why their leader
—their Scoutmaster—should have considerable experience of life
and should himself know something of its difficulties and its dis-
appointments.

The Chief Scout has written : " Unselfishness, self-discipline,
wider fellow-feeling, sense of honour and duty should be implanted,
and such attributes as enable a man, *no matter what his standing*, to
look beyond his own immediate ledger or bench to see the good of his
work for the community, putting into his routine some service for
others as well as for himself, developing also some perception of
what is beautiful in nature, in art and in literature, so that his
higher interests may be aroused, and he may get enjoyment from
his surroundings, whatever they may be. These are points of
which we in the Scout Movement can do so much to impart the
elements and to lay the foundations."

It is such passages as these that make the average Scouter wonder
whether he is fitted for the work he has undertaken. The very fact
of his wonder may be taken as a sign that he has the possibilities
of being a good Scoutmaster in him.

A word may be said of the basis of the Scout system of training
which is commonly cited as " expression as opposed to impression." It encourages self-development on the part of each
individual boy, and, as we have already discovered, lays special

emphasis in the first place on the development of character and initiative. In other words, instead of instructing our boys we try and get them, by encouragement, to learn for themselves. The Scouter's work is merely to give to the boy the ambition and desire to learn for himself by suggesting to him activities which interest him, or which will interest him because of the way in which they are presented. That is where Romance and Adventure come in. That is why the first sentence of *Scouting for Boys* says : " By the term ' scouting ' is meant the work and attributes of back-woodsmen, explorers and frontiersmen."

Briefly our system is to lead the boys on to pass tests in badge qualifications, handicrafts, and so on, for which they may have an —as yet—undiscovered natural bent, or which may be of value to them in the future ; to encourage manliness by tests in swimming, pioneering, athletics, camping, journeys ; to encourage personal responsibility in a boy for his own health and physical and moral well-being ; to develop character and self-reliance by the Patrol System ; to place trust in a Scout's honour ; to give him the benefit of high ideals ; and, we trust, in most Troops, to give him the benefit of friendly and personal advice at those stages of his development when he is most in need of a helping hand.

Scouting is not " a school having a definite curriculum and stan-dard of examinations," nor is it " a brigade of officers and privates for drilling manliness into boys."

Scouting is not a military movement ; it entails no collective instruction, but individual education. To achieve the latter it is essential that the attitude of the Scouter to his Scouts should be emphatically that of the " elder brother," with all the love of family and firmness that that title implies. It is his duty to study the character of each of his boys, to make himself acquainted with their home environment so that he will be able to suggest interests to them which will enable them to develop their own characters and abilities and to reach the goal of education—

" No man can be called educated who has not a willingness and a desire, as well as a trained ability, to do his part in the world's work."

BOOKS.

*Scouting for Boys*, Baden-Powell. Pearson, 2s. 6d. and 4s.
*Aids to Scoutmastership*, Baden-Powell. Jenkins, 2s.

## CHAPTER III

### THE FOUNDATIONS OF THE BUILDING

IF any Scouter is going to make a real success of his job—by that I mean if he is going to have any lasting influence on the boys who come under his leadership—it is absolutely necessary that he should be quite clear in his own mind what the real basis of Scouting is. I have no hesitation in saying that the whole foundation of Scouting rests upon the Scout Law and the Scout Promise and the meaning and spirit that they carry with them. The Law and the Promise should set the tone to the whole of a boy's Scout life, which, it is to be sincerely hoped, he will intermingle with his normal life as boy and man so that the two are indistinguishable.

The Scout Law and the Scout Promise are among the first points in Scouting that a boy learns ; they should be made to appear to him as the most important.

The Scouter himself must appreciate their importance, and must set himself to master their inner meaning, since it is for him to convey some idea of their significance to his boys.

### The Scout Law

It is only possible to touch upon the Scout Law generally and, I am afraid, very inadequately. Have we ever really set ourselves down to consider that Law, and tried to come to a clear understanding of what it means, of what it entails ? Each Scouter must appreciate the fact that the Law applies to him personally, as well as to his Scouts, that he himself has to live up to it as best he can so that he may set an example to his Scouts. It is by our own personal example that we can lead boys to be good citizens ; how important is it, then, that we should try to be good citizens ourselves at all times.

It is not sufficient that either we or our Scouts should know the Scout Law in the sense that we can repeat it like parrots whenever required, although many of us would fail even at that test. Much more is necessary. We must know what it really means.

We can find various interpretations of each Law in the Chief Scout's writings, in Roland Philipps' *Letters to a Patrol Leader*, in Chapter XX of Dr. Griffin's *The Quest of the Boy*. I have no desire to repeat what these three have already said. What I want to emphasise now is that the Scout Law is the vital foundation on which the whole building of Scouting rests, and to try and induce a right attitude towards it.

Many writers and speakers have said that the Scout Law represents an impossible ideal. It is an ideal, but by no means impossible, for is not an ideal an aim that rises higher the closer

B

we approach like successive peaks in a mountain range ? In giving us the Law the Chief Scout has gathered together within a small compass much of the moral code of the world throughout the centuries. He has expressed it in a positive way ; he has placed standards before the boy for him to try and achieve ; he has given him a challenge, not a chiding ; an encouragement, not a forbiddance.

Further than that, the Scout Law has been worded in such a way that the boy, if his Scouter will only allow him, can understand what is implied by it. The Law holds a direct appeal to him, because all the factors which it contains are familiar in everyday life. Too often Scouters make the mistake of explaining too much, of introducing illustrations which only grown-ups could appreciate, with the result that they leave the boy fogged and uncertain. Sometimes Scouters go to the other extreme where bad is worse confounded, and make no mention of the Law to their Troop or to any Scout once he has passed his Tenderfoot tests.

Some explanation is necessary, but let it be a simple and natural one. Let the Patrol Leaders help here too. I agree that the Scoutmaster should go through the Law with each of his new fellows, but he should not thereby deprive his Patrol Leaders and any would-be First-class Scout of their part in the training of the recruit. I have known many a Patrol Leader who could explain the Scout Law to a youngster better than any grown-up. He can show the Law to be a matter of everyday interest, whereas the Scouter may make it unnatural by his very words.

Not only must we lay our foundations carefully, we must also see to it that nothing interferes with them afterwards, that they are not endangered by insidious outside influences or internal decay. We must, therefore, try and keep the Law before our Scouts in the ordinary everyday doings of the Troop, and of their lives at home and at school. Encourage them to set up a copy of the Law in their own homes ; have it emblazoned in their Troop Headquarters, even if the scroll has to be taken down and removed after every meeting ; bring it into your yarns from time to time, not only at a Scouts' Own, as a matter of everyday life and conversation. Encourage each Scout's efforts to live up to the Law, help him in his difficulties—that is one of our greatest privileges —cheer him on in his struggle, help him to get his parents and friends to realise what it all means to him.

When talking to the Troop or to an individual Scout it is unwise to lay too much stress on the difficulties they may experience in keeping the Law. Try and get them to understand that the ideals expressed by the Law are natural ones, which they can accept and live up to. They will meet with difficulties, especially the older ones amongst them. Others that they will encounter in their work have let such ideals fall into disuse, if they ever knew about them at all, but they have done so because they have had no one

to help them, no brother Scout to stand at their backs and give
them strength.   It is from the Brotherhood of Scouts that we can
all draw strength to preserve our ideals undimmed.

The Scout Law points out the right way through life, and it
does stand for a high ideal.   But, just because it represents such
a high ideal—an ideal which is very often beyond the reach of us
imperfect human beings—we should remember that the Promise
which all Scouts make—men, women and boys—is that we *will
do our best* to keep the Scout Law.   We may break it at times,
but, when we do, we should realise that we are not to give up in
despair, but are expected to keep on trying to do our best again
and again to keep the Scout Law.   We are held responsible to
ourselves for our thoughts, our words, our deeds.

If we Scouters, in our poor, imperfect way, can by our example
impress these facts on our Scouts, we have set their faces towards
the great adventure—the quest of a clean and upright life.

### The Scout Promise

The Scout Promise, in practically identically the same form, is
the affirmation that is required of all—men, women and boys—
before they can become members of the world-wide Scout Brotherhood.   I am aware that this is not always the case with some
Scouters ; all I need say is that no one who has not taken the Promise
is entitled to consider himself a Scout or to wear a Scout badge.
It should be quite obvious that when the boy is asked to enter
into a solemn obligation, the men who are working with him should
accept the same obligation.

The Promise is the source from which the whole of our Scouting springs, it is the force which gives it life.   Like the Law it
represents a high ideal ; an ideal, as I have already said, which is
made possible by our promise to do our best.   Before he makes
his Promise and at the Investiture Ceremony itself each boy
should be reminded of that qualification, and reminded, too, that
he is not alone in his endeavours, but has all other Scouts to help
him.

When we make the Scout Promise on our honour, we pledge
our own personal reputation that we will do our best to be upright
and straight in all our dealings.   Our honour is a bright shield
that we have to keep free from stain.   All the best of chivalry is
ready to our hand to illustrate this point to our Scouts.   So that
even in the Scout Promise there lies an appeal to Romance and
Adventure ;  it is not such a solemn, dull thing after all.

The next phrase—" to do my duty to God and the King "—
contains two complete and distinct parts.   Duty to God is obviously of extreme importance and is purposely set in the fore-
front.   It is the foundation-stone on which the whole of Scouting
is built, the mortar which binds the whole fabric of Scouting together.   While our conception of duty to God may differ in details

it remains the same in principle and consists in making the best possible use of the gifts that God has given us in ourselves, in the people with whom we come in contact, and in the great world round about us. Scouting itself is one of these gifts and should be kept spotless and untarnished, but increased so that it can be passed on to others as well.

The question of religion and Scouting's policy in connection with it will be discussed elsewhere, together with the ways in which the Scouter can help boys in their spiritual welfare. Now I will merely add that it is essential for each Scouter to realise the vital nature of this part of the Promise, and to realise that he himself is expected to subscribe to it, and that he cannot conscientiously be a member of the Scout Brotherhood unless he believes in God.

Duty to the King is a question of loyalty. Scouting takes its stand on the side of established order. The Chief Scout wrote at some length on this question in *The Scouter* for August, 1926, and I reproduce some of his remarks here :

" My own belief, is that we are seeing only the beginning of the Empire coming into its full strength and power as a beneficent organisation for ensuring peace in the world. The British States, though independent in their administration, are interdependent in commerce. Wars in the past have put to the test their self-sacrificing loyalty to one another and to the Mother Country. That Mother Country fostered them until they could run alone, so that now, while able to manage their own affairs, and to make their own life like sons in a family, they still preserve the bond of blood and still look to the King as their joint head.

" So long as they do this they will be a commonwealth of federal nations, distributed over every part of the globe and having a joint power such as never before existed in history. But it is a power of which the nations of the world need have no fear. It will be a power for the peace and prosperity of all. As a ' nation of shop-keepers,' war is not in our line, so ' to do our duty to the King,' as enjoined on Scouts and Guides, means that Scouters and Guiders should inculcate this idea of the British Commonwealth into the oncoming generation in our respective countries, and, what is more, we should urge them in their turn to impress it on their children for the good of all.

" Therefore, we must so shape our training with the right vision that we shall not be content merely to have smart Troops and temporary success, but we must be sure that the highest ideals have been actually inculcated, and that the boys and girls really bring a Christian spirit into their daily lives and practices ; that they overcome selfishness with service, and that they substitute goodwill and co-operation for the too-prevalent state of narrow patriotism and jealousies."

Unselfishness is another quality that Scouting stands for, and so the Scout promises to do his best " to help other people at all times." The daily " good turn " teaches the habit of unselfishness. A boy has a natural instinct for good, if only he knows how to exercise it, and the daily good turn and the encouragement he should receive from his Scoutmaster develop this instinct. The doing of things for other people is emphasised through all the stages of his Scout training—in the Second- and First-class tests, in the teaching of first-aid, life-saving, public health, pathfinding. The King's Scout Badge is designed to set the seal on his ability to do services for other people. The means are ready to hand if the Scouter will only see them and utilise them.

Lastly the Scout promises to do his best to keep the Scout Law. That there is a permissive alteration of the Scout Promise for Scouters—" to carry out the spirit of the Scout Law "—does not seem to me to be necessary. Both wordings imply precisely the same thing, the keeping and guarding of the Scout Law being possibly even more complete than the other expression. Speaking personally, I believe that all Scouters who can should take the Scout Promise in the same form as they ask their boys to take it.

### The Scout Spirit

In *The Spirit of Scouting* Maurice Gamon, who is associated with Roland Philipps and Anthony Slingsby in the minds of many Scouters whose memories go back to the days before the Great War, described the Scout Spirit as made up of self-reliance, self-sacrifice and self-control. The Scout Spirit was the thing in the whole Scout Movement for which these three lived and longed and worked. The three attributes mentioned go to the making up of a boy's and man's character.

The liberty and individuality of Scouting allow and encourage the Scout to learn self-reliance.

Through the expected performance of at least one good turn a day the Scout gradually, but surely, acquires the habit of self-sacrifice. The history of every religion and of every country furnishes him with examples to follow.

Through devotion to the Scout Law the Scout learns the art of self-control. Through his games and practices he puts that art into effective use so that it is strengthened to meet the demands that will be made of it in later years.

It is imperative that the Scouter should set about his work fully determined to produce the results that are intended. It is not a matter of outward show or display, but the formation of character that is important. The Scout Spirit should be the underlying influence which pervades the whole of his work, which pervades the whole of the Scouting that is done in his Troop.

In *Scouting for Boys* the Chief has appealed to the boy's gift for hero-worship, his love of adventure and romance, and his all-embracing love of play, but he has welded these three component parts together by the aid of the Scout Spirit ; if that spirit is absent, the intricate machine which he has built up for us to use will not move.

We build our foundations below the surface, and we must look below the surface for them. Once the building is accomplished we must not dismiss them from our minds, the whole building is dependent on them for its stability. We must never forget.

BOOKS.

*The Patrol System and Letters to a Patrol Leader*, Philipps. Pearson, 2s. 6d. (Three separate books, 6d. each.)

*The Quest of the Boy*, Griffin. Faith Press, 1s. 6d.

*The Spirit of Scouting*, Gamon. Pilgrim Press, 8d.

CHAPTER IV

BEGINNING TO BUILD

Now that we have decided what we are aiming at in our building and have laid our foundations it is possible to start on the construction.

To commence with it is obviously necessary to collect the essential tools. Starting from the assumption that someone who has not been connected with Scouting before has decided to start a Troop, it is possible to give some definite advice which will be of use to such a person, and may also help others who already have some experience, or who are joining an existing Troop.

The Boy Scouts Association publishes from 25 Buckingham Palace Road, London, S.W.1, a pamphlet entitled *How to start a Troop*, which contains information on the subject. It is possibly advisable to state here certain definitions with which that pamphlet commences :

" A complete Scout Group consists of the following three sections : Cub Pack, Scout Troop and Rover Scout Crew, but may at any given time consist of one or more sections only. (*Rule* 9.)

" A Scout Troop is one of the sections of a Scout Group, and is under the charge of a Scoutmaster, with at least one Assistant Scoutmaster to ensure continuity. (Each Group must have a Group Scoutmaster eventually.)

" A Troop is divided into Patrols consisting of six to eight Scouts, including Patrol Leader and Second. The Patrol should be the unit in all competitions,˙ and the formation of specialised Patrols is recommended. It is usually found best to have Patrols of six rather than of seven or eight.

" If the Troop consists of more than three Patrols, an additional Assistant Scoutmaster is advisable for every three Patrols or fraction thereof. (*See Rule* 11.) "

Our would-be Scouter now knows what he is after. The various points that are mentioned in this quotation, such as Patrols and Assistant Scoutmasters, will be discussed later on ; now we are more concerned with the tools our hero—for he may be a real hero to start Scouting in some parts of the country even to-day—should select for his first building operations.

First and foremost comes *Scouting for Boys* by the Chief Scout —now Lord Baden-Powell of Gilwell. This book contains the principles which underlie Scouting. It is the motive power which caused boys and men to take up Scouting in 1908, and it is the Scouts' and Scouters' chief aid to inspiration to-day. It is worth remembering that Patrols and Troops sprang up all over the country simply and solely because some boy or man had procured the fortnightly parts of *Scouting for Boys,* had read them, had collected some of his pals, or some boys in his neighbourhood, together, and had set out to put into practice some of the principles and methods about which he had read. The book can be of the same value to-day, not only to would-be Scouters starting new Troops, but also to existing Scouters working with well-established Troops. The more it can be read by man and boy in Scouting the better.

To the uninitiated this book on Scouting may not appear to be sufficiently definite. He is not told by it what to do at all stages of his work. That is why I have deliberately labelled it a tool. It is the earliest and best tool to take into our hands and to use according to our good judgment and understanding. A sculptor uses a chisel, but he does not expect that chisel to stand up and tell him how to use it. The Chief Scout's intention was to supply an aid to Scouting, not a manual containing orders and regulations.

There is, however, another tool available, which may be likened to the mallet that directs the chisel along the right lines. That tool is a book entitled *Policy, Organisation, and Rules,* procurable at a cost of 6d. from the Imperial Headquarters of the Boy Scouts Association. This book should be obtained, and at least Part I of it read and digested, as well as those portions of Parts II and III—Organisation and Ranks—which refer to Scout Troops and Scouts. Don't be put off by the seemingly large number of rules ; remember that they deal with all aspects of Scouting ; and pay particular attention to the Chief Scout's sub-title : " Rules on how to play the Game of Scouting for Boys."

These two tools will be needed throughout the whole of our Scout work—not only at the beginning. They should be in constant use, and that constant use will ensure that we set about our Scouting in the right spirit and conduct it along right lines.

At this early stage it is necessary to get into touch with the local Scout Commissioner and Scout Secretary, whose addresses can always be obtained on application to Imperial Headquarters or the various National Headquarters. Obviously it is an act of courtesy, if nothing else, to inform the existing Scout authorities of your intentions, while they can give you a considerable amount of information and help. If it is not possible to get into personal touch with them, then every effort should be made to seek the advice of some neighbouring Scoutmaster. It is advisable to try and get to see the actual working of a good Troop. That, too, is always advisable, however much experience we may already have had in Scouting. If we make a point of trying to gather practical experience from as many different quarters as possible, our own Scout work is bound to improve.

### *" Open " or " Controlled " Groups*

When a new Group is being started, a decision has to be made as to whether it is open or controlled. Rules 2 and 9 set out clearly the nature and effect of a Group being controlled. It is unnecessary here to go fully into the pros and cons of the question, but in thinly populated areas it is desirable to see that the Group is not restricted in any way. If the number of boys in the district is small, and only certain boys are allowed to become Scouts, the others are precluded from Scouting since there are not sufficient numbers to justify the existence of two separate Groups. In urban districts very much will depend on local circumstances. All Scouters of a controlled Group should, however, be careful to get to know and understand the obligations which are placed on them. This is necessary even when a Group has been in existence for some considerable time.

### *Headquarters*

When it has been decided to start a Troop as the beginnings of a complete Scout Group and some knowledge of Scouting has been acquired, the next step to take is to find some kind of a meeting-place where the Scouts can gather together. One of the qualifications of a Scoutmaster is the ability to obtain the use of some sort of clubroom for Scout meetings. It is true that in the early days many a Patrol and Troop was formed round a lamp-post, and real Scouting was done despite the absence of any headquarters. To-day, however, it is absolutely impossible to hope for any success unless a room is available. At first quite a small room will be sufficient—an old cellar, store or loft will make an effective meeting-place for the few boys who are first collected together. A schoolroom or a church hall can be made to do, but suffers obviously from the disadvantages of not being the possession of the Scouts. It is a mistake to use a hall, where the presence of Scouts is sometimes only suffered, because it is large in preference to a small room of your own. Lack of space is a handicap from the point of view of games and other practices, but existence on sufferance is a much more serious handicap from the point of view of atmosphere and Scout spirit. More consideration will be given to Scout headquarters later on from the point of view of their use and decoration ; at present we are only concerned with the need for some kind of a meeting-place. From the very beginning, however, try and secure something that is attractive, well lighted and ventilated, easily warmed, or capable of being heated cheaply, and, if possible, apart from dwelling houses. A certain amount of noise is involved in real live Scouting, and if the Scouts have continuously to go about on tip-toe and speak in whispers, their interest is practically bound to die away.

## Making a Start

When building a house brick is laid alongside brick, course is laid on course, and it is precisely the same kind of procedure we must adopt in building up a Scout Troop. We have to go about our job carefully and gradually. It is of vital importance to commence with small numbers.

Definite permission to start the Group, or to add a Scout Troop to one or other sections of an existing Group, should be obtained from the local Commissioner and local Scout Association Secretary. When it is properly founded it will be registered at Imperial Headquarters.

However you eventually start the Troop, it is generally best to issue a general invitation to likely boys to meet and discuss the possibilities. The gathering should be as cheerful as you can make it—cocoa, for instance, is useful in dispelling shyness, but should not be used as a bribe ! At this preliminary gathering a short talk about Scouting should be given, care being taken to explain that while Scouting gives boys a great deal of pleasure and fun and interesting activities, yet there is a serious side to it, which their fathers and mothers at any rate will be able to appreciate. It is best to lay special emphasis on the fact that slackers are not wanted, and that each boy who joins the Troop must be prepared to do his bit to make the Troop a thoroughly good one. All those who desire to become Scouts should then be asked to give in their names.

The next step depends somewhat on personal taste and on local opinion. Six or so of the boys who appear likely to become leaders can be accepted at once and their training as Tenderfoot Scouts commenced. This is the course I would personally follow, unless circumstances seemed obviously to dictate an alternative. The alternative is to accept all those who offer, provided there are not more than twenty, and to start the Troop with them.

The larger numbers will obviously increase initial difficulties, but it may not be possible nor politic to make any distinction at first between the volunteers. It is, however, quite impossible to start any Troop and hope to conduct it on Scout lines with more than twenty at first.

Very frequently it does no harm to keep some boys out for two or three months, and it is a good thing if admission is not made too easy.

However small numbers may be it is extremely advisable to secure someone as an assistant in order to ensure continuity of work, to take your place in any absence from illness or otherwise, and to secure that personal individual attention is given to each boy. It is also important to secure the written permission of the parents or guardians of the boys you accept. If you have been able to get into direct touch with them, or have had an opportunity of letting them know what Scouting is, so much the better. There are several leaflets available which will help you here.

### Patrol Leaders

If the first alternative has been adopted, some of these first six boys or so may, but not necessarily must, become the Patrol Leaders as the Troop grows. It is generally advisable not to appoint Patrol Leaders at the very beginning. It is possible to try out the older boys one after another by putting a different boy at the head of the Patrol each successive week. In this way an idea can be obtained as to which boys are likely to make good leaders over the others. This is the same in whatever way a start has been made.

If the Troop grows gradually in numbers, the most promising of the first few boys can be appointed as Leaders after they have passed their Tenderfoot tests and have been invested as Scouts and are on the way to become Second-class Scouts

It is quite obvious that in a voluntary movement such as Scouting a man or boy can only lead if he has more knowledge and experience than those he sets out to lead. That is an important point for all Scouters to remember.

In the very beginning, since Scout traditions must be slow in coming at first, it is best for the Scoutmaster to appoint the Patrol Leaders and Seconds. Thereafter it is possible to leave the selection to the Court of Honour, or to the Patrols themselves. In such cases voting should be by ballot, which must be kept secret, and it must be understood that the Scoutmaster will not necessarily appoint the boy with the most votes if he considers him unsuitable.

To many this Chapter will appear to be of a very elementary nature, but it would be inadvisable to omit mention of the early stages of our building, because a great deal depends on them. If a bad start has been made, it will prove very difficult to secure good Scouting thereafter. There have been many cases where long-existing Troops have had to demolish all that they have done and start again. While even in comparatively good Scout Troops reconstruction is from time to time necessary and advisable. So it is that even Scouters of long experience may benefit from some of the simple hints herein contained.

BOOK.
*Policy, Organisation and Rules*, I.H.Q., 6d.

## CHAPTER V

### MATERIALS TO USE

WHEN a building is constructed the materials to be used are selected with great care, and the wise builder realises to the full that, if he wishes his building to stand up against storm and shine, he must be particularly careful to see that only the best materials go to the building of it. These materials are frequently the outcome of past experience ; practical and scientific tests are made ; durability is watched and tested ; suitability for the soil and situation is taken into account.

In the same way we want to avoid jerry-building in our Scout Troops. We are building for the future, and we do not desire our building to collapse at the first sign of storm. We desire that our Troop should go on from year to year firm and straight and strong. We desire that each member of the Troop should continue as a Scout for the rest of his life, that he should stand as a Scout in actions and principles, even if not in name. It matters not whether we call a house a bungalow or a mansion, so long as it is a sound, comfortable, happy and healthy dwelling-place. It matters not whether we call a fellow a Scout or a Rover Scout or a Scouter— or none of these names—so long as he sticks to the aims and principles that he has learnt as a Scout earlier on, and does his best to carry them out in life.

And so to our materials in Scouting.

The first sentence of the first chapter of *Scouting for Boys* reads : " Instruction in Scouting should be given as far as possible through practices, games and competitions." These are materials which have been tried out scientifically and practically in the past, and are warranted sound. It is the doing of things that is such an important feature of the Scouting programme. From the very beginning both Scouters and Scouts should realise and appreciate this important factor.

Sometimes with a new Troop it is difficult to stand aside and see the boys making mistakes. The Hadow Report on " The Education of the Adolescent " tells us that " A boy will have missed much of the value of school life unless he has had many opportunities of making mistakes. It is far better that a match be lost than that overzealous watchfulness should leave nothing to the initiative of the taught. It is far easier for the teacher to interfere too much than to stand aside and watch, only taking a hand himself to avert catastrophe. There should be small catastrophes if the proper training is to be given."

Even to-day many a Scoutmaster makes the mistake of doing things for himself because they can be done easier and quicker that way, but, despite his arguments, his Scouts will not learn just from watching him, nor will they be much interested in his activities. Apart from that he is depriving them of all the excitement of the game, of doing these things that interest them for themselves, of making their own mistakes—for there is fun in making mistakes. Sometimes it is just selfishness on the Scouter's part. He likes cooking, and so he enjoys himself and at the same time can tell ignorant people how self-sacrificing he is.

Apart from all that, if a Scoutmaster is to occupy himself with the details of Scouting, to do everything for his boys instead of with them, he is going to leave himself no time for his real job in Scouting—the training of the characters of his boys.

So let us make use of these materials that the Chief Scout suggested in the beginning and that the passage of years has proved sound. As we carry on with our building these materials will be mentioned from time to time, but in the beginning we would do well to pay special attention to the subject of games.

*Games*

We could very easily and with advantage devote a whole chapter to this subject, but other aspects of our Scouting might suffer thereby. All these materials which we use in our Scouting have got to be utilised in their proper proportions. If, for instance, we play games to the exclusion of everything else, our Troop will become a games club and not a Scout Troop. If, on the other hand, we leave games out of our programmes altogether, our Troop is in danger of becoming an extension class where the boys have no opportunities of healthy enjoyment.

There is no need to be ashamed of using games in our training. The early realisation of their educative use is one of the triumphs of Scouting and of its Founder. In making use of games we are utilising a natural method of self-development such as we see exemplified by the kitten that chases a ball of wool, or the dog that races madly round the lawn. By a judicious use and selection of games we can further not only the physical and mental development of the boy, but also his moral and spiritual development.

On the other hand we have got to be particularly careful not to overdo it, and let our Scouting degenerate into games and nothing but games. A certain amount of real work is essential to character building. In fact the virtue of real hard work was never more necessary than it is to-day, and each Scouter should endeavour to show the joy and happiness that can be got out of sticking to a job, even a dirty one, until it has been accomplished. If through our games and practices we can convey an idea of the dignity of labour we will have achieved a great deal of our purpose.

There should be no difficulty in acquiring a sufficient stock of games. Many varieties will be found in *Scouting for Boys* and in the other books, while the pages of *The Scouter* and the good graces of one's fellow-Scouters are fruitful sources of inspiration.

There is a sentence in *Gilcraft's Book of Games* that is worth repeating :

" In games, as in everything else in Scouting, local conditions play a very important part, and the Scouter who is using games as a key to the padlock of the boys' characters, must realise this to the full, and be prepared to make alterations in rules and conditions, to drop out conditions which are unsuitable, to combine games together in one, and to suit his programme of games to his programme of other Scout activities."

Although to the boy the game may appear merely a matter of recreation and enjoyment, the Scouter must realise that it has a definite purpose in his scheme of character training, and not fall into the habit of just playing any old game merely for the sake of playing a game.

A few practical hints will not come amiss. First and foremost insist on every game being played in the best possible spirit. See that everyone understands what is wanted before they start. Give the Patrol Leaders an opportunity of finding out about the rules of a new game beforehand, and give them an opportunity of seeing that their Patrols understand. Physical games and inter-Patrol Games should start with the Patrols in some recognised order and formation, and the Scouts should start and finish in a certain recognised position. A few moments at the Alert is an aid to self-discipline. No one should be left out of it ; those not playing should be asked to help with the collection and distribution of gear, as markers, or even as judges. The one exception is the Scoutmaster, who would be well advised to stand aside sometimes when games are being played and just watch how the Patrols and individual Scouts set about it. He is watching form—and that means character.

See that variety is introduced both in the types of games and in the actual games used to illustrate these types. To this end some kind of a record should be kept, and care taken to consult it when building up a programme and also to see that the games played fit in with the work done, either by way of variety or by way of illustration. " Finally remember that games are only useful when they are subordinate to the general scheme of Scouting. If they overshadow other Scouting, then they become a menace."

## The Patrol System

For team games of all kinds the Patrol naturally forms a handy unit, but this is not the only value of the division of a Troop into Patrols. When the first Scout camp was conducted in 1907, the Chief divided the boys who attended into four Patrols under their own Leaders, and all the work of the camp was conducted in accordance with what is now known as the Patrol System, a system that was explained and expounded by Roland Philipps in his book *The Patrol System*. Briefly the idea is that the Troop should be self-governing, that the Scouts themselves should have some say in the workings of it, that they should be trained to be self-reliant through the opportunities afforded them of exercising leadership and control, that, as we have already learned, they should profit from their own mistakes.

It is true that the idea came to the Chief in the Army and that he further developed it in the South African Constabulary, but it is almost diametrically opposed to normal military methods.

We all know that boys consort together in gangs, just as in later life men and women consort together in cliques or clubs. In our own boyhood we can remember the joy and advantage we gained out of going about with our own little band, the things we did, the escapades we performed. The Patrol is just such a band turned to good account to further the well-being of the Troop and the cause of Scouting.

The exact composition of our Patrols depends very much on circumstances. The natural gang is a desirable aim, but is not always capable of attainment. Other things being equal, however, it is advantageous to associate friends together in the same Patrol. If the Troop is drawn from a wide area it is obviously better to associate the boys from one small district in the same Patrol, as they may have opportunities of gathering together as a Patrol on their own, which is very desirable.

The question of age is also a difficult one which can only be decided according to the circumstances of the case. If a Patrol is all of an age there is a possibility of their being more together, though this is not always borne out in practice. There is, however, more possibility of their being more or less at the same standard of Scouting, so that their activities can be of a more corporate nature. On the other hand, when a Patrol ranges in age from Patrol Leader to Tenderfoot there are more possibilities of the older Scouts gaining experience of leadership and responsibility in the training of the younger Scouts.

It is the character-training value of the Patrol System that to my mind is the most important. The Patrol should be a real live factor in the Troop, not just a matter of form. The greater part of the boys' training should be done through the Patrol and the Patrol Leaders. Even if the Scoutmaster is doubtful about their efficiency, still he must delegate authority to them and give them some responsibility and opportunities of exercising leadership. More will be said on the subject of Patrol Leaders later ; now it is sufficient to say that they must be trusted if anything is to be made of them or of their Patrols. Experience is one of the best teachers there is—not the S.M.—and only by real trial can the leaders of the boys be tested and they themselves grow in strength.

The Court of Honour is an integral part of the Patrol System, but that again will be dealt with later.

And now a word or two as to the effect of it all. I have already indicated that this delegation of authority, so to speak, secures the association of the boys themselves in the traditions and doings of the Troop. We have also seen that the Patrol Method is an essential part of the Scout Method in so far as character training is concerned. Apart from all that, with the system in proper working order, the Scoutmaster is relieved of an immense amount of routine work. He himself is in close personal contact with his Patrol Leaders so far as their Scout training is concerned. They in their turn pass on that training to the boys in their Patrols, thus ensuring personal contact. Despite this, however, the Scoutmaster and other Scouters in the Troop are able to treat each member of the Troop as an individual, and since their attention is not all required for details, they are able to give consideration to the broader and more important aspects of Scouting and to set each individual boy on the road to good citizenship.

In a later chapter more will be said of the functions of Patrol Leaders and of the comradeship that should exist between them and the Scouters. One danger may be pointed out now, for forewarned is forearmed. Sometimes it happens that a Patrol gets above itself, that the Patrol spirit is allowed to rise too high. From the very beginning it should be plainly understood by all concerned that the Patrols merge in the Troop, that the whole is greater than the part, that a real good Troop spirit must be obtained and preserved. There is no clash of loyalties. The individual Scout strives after Scout efficiency in order that his Patrol may benefit ; the Patrol strives to attain a high standard in order that the Troop as a whole may progress.

## PAMPHLETS.

(Available, free of charge, on application to the Secretary, The Boy Scouts Association, 25, Buckingham Palace Road, London, S.W.1.)

*About Those Boy Scouts.* A holograph letter written and illustrated by the Chief Scout.

*Twelve Good Reasons why your Boy should become a Scout.*

*What shall I do with my Boy?* A letter to Parents.

*When You're a Scout.* Containing a Message to Parents and a Form of Application for membership.

*The Scouter.* The Headquarters Gazette of the Boy Scouts Association, annual subscription, 4s. 6d., post paid, The Manager, *The Scouter*, 18 Henrietta Street, London, W.C. 2.

## BOOKS.

*Scouting Games*, Baden-Powell. Pearson, 1s. 6d. and 2s. 6d.

*Gilcraft's Book of Games.* Pearson, 1s. 6d. and 2s. 6d. (This book contains references to many other games books.)

## CHAPTER VI

### BEAMS AND GIRDERS

WE have by no means exhausted the list of materials that we should have ready to hand all through the erection of our Scout building. In fact the list is almost inexhaustible since all's grist that comes to the Scout mill. It is one of the peculiar features of Scouting that it is able to afford scope for good work to all kinds of men and women, no matter what their upbringing, training or experience may have been, since Scouting can find a place for their peculiar talents whatever they may be. This is an important point to remember. There is no hard and fast rule of Scouting ; so long as its main aims and methods are grasped, it is possible to arrive somewhere near these aims by very diverse methods.

### Individuality

It is the individual who counts, whose interests should be served. This refers both to Scouts and Scouters. The Scouter can only set about his task according to his own tastes, after he is satisfied that his tastes are in general keeping with the principles he is asked to follow. His personality must be taken into account, and counts for a very great deal. As Dean Russell of Columbia University indicated in a famous address about Scouting, " The naturalist may praise it for its success in putting the boy close to nature's heart ; the moralist, for its splendid code of ethics ; the hygienist, for its methods of physical training ; the parent, for its ability to keep the boy out of mischief."

But it is not only the individuality of the Scouter that is concerned ; the individuality of the Scouts themselves is of equal importance. In order to make for success in his real job the Scouter must treat each single Scout as a separate problem, he must do his best to supply his needs and desires, while at the same time he endeavours to cater for the requirements of the Troop as a whole. This question of individual study and treatment is dealt with in a pamphlet published by I.H.Q. entitled *Tracking Rules for Scouters*, where certain well-known tracking rules are applied to the question of character training.

It is necessary for all of us, however, to make as much use as possible of individual treatment in our Scout work, and for this reason, apart from any other, the numbers in any one Troop should always be restricted. In *Scouting for Boys* the Chief Scout suggests thirty-two as a maximum number for individual training.

### Discipline

Another material of which we will need to make great use is discipline. There are several kinds of poor qualities on the market, and we have to be very careful from the outset as to the actual brand that we choose. The need for some kind of discipline in any kind of work is obvious. There is just as much need for it in Scouting as in anything else. If we are training boys to be good citizens, we have to train them to recognise that some kind of order is essential to progress.

Sometimes we talk glibly of discipline from within as opposed to discipline from without, overlooking two important considerations : First, that self-discipline, as it is called, is not the prerogative of Scouting alone, it is the ideal aimed at in life generally ; second, that if discipline is to grow from within it must need some encouragement from without. It is like a plant. First of all the soil is prepared, then the seed is planted ; the ground is watered and other artificial aids are applied to encourage the seed to grow. When the first shoots appear they are carefully watched lest a sudden frost nips them ; as the plant continues to grow it is tended, withered leaves are removed, perhaps it is staked to give it strength to stand upright. It is much the same with discipline, it needs care and attention, it is not fair to leave it all to itself to withstand the buffets of the weather. Too frequently the expression self-discipline, or discipline from within, is used by the faint-hearted Scouter as an excuse for having no discipline of any kind.

A complete review of the subject will be found in another I.H.Q. pamphlet, *Discipline in the Scout Movement*, and it is from that pamphlet that the following paragraphs are taken :

" So far as Scouting is concerned, Discipline is not an end in itself, but is a road to general well-being. Every member of the Scout Brotherhood, from latest joined Tenderpad to the Chief Scout himself, is ever mindful of the happiness and comfort of his companions, and, rather than do anything detrimental to the common welfare, he will without any hesitation suppress any desires and wishes of his own. That is our Aim.

" So far as the individual Cub or Scout or Rover Scout is concerned, the object of the Scouter's teaching of discipline is in the interests of the boy, not in the interests of the Scouter.

" The keynote then of the lead to be given in regard to discipline from the outside is sympathy. The word is derived from the Greek, and means ' to feel with.' The Scouter must feel with his boys, he must place himself in their position, he must see things through their eyes, he must grasp their point of view, their thoughts, their feelings, their difficulties. The Scouter must be a Cub or a Scout or a Rover himself first of all in spirit. He himself should be inspired by an ideal—the ideal of the highest form of leadership that it is possible to conceive.

" The attitude the Scouter should adopt towards his Scouts is one of complete trust—confident belief in his boys. If nothing else did, our First Scout Law places that obligation upon us. Out of a somewhat wider experience than Scouting, I can assure you that the policy of trust is the best possible policy anyone can adopt in any walk of life. With such an attitude towards them,

c

and in such an atmosphere, the Scouts will rise to the highest level to which they can attain."

These are the ethics of the subject. A practical exposition of the methods that can be adopted, and more especially of the methods to be avoided, is set out in the pamphlet. It would take too long for me to detail them here.

There is one other consideration, and that is that in Scouting, Scouters are privileged to help. Their job is to scout *with* boys, to take the boys into their confidence, to give them opportunities to make suggestions, to select their own activities within reason. Such an attitude on the Scouters' part must make for the right kind of atmosphere and of discipline. Any kind of over-riding, autocratic methods on the part of a Scouter will have the same effect as a virulent poison. On the other hand, casualness and weakness will have the same ultimate result. If we had no experience in our own boyhood, we all need to learn the true functions of an " elder brother." These did not include sentimentality or softness, but a guardianship of the family honour which was emphasised by considerable firmness of control. Those of us who have been fortunate enough to have real elder brothers of our own realise the debt we owe them for the forming of our characters.

### Romance

Half the success of Scouting lies in the atmosphere which can be obtained in the Troop. This is really dependent on the way we set about our job. If we can induce a spirit of adventure and romance into all that we do, then we will build well. In order to see how this can be done I would ask you to look at *Scouting for Boys* and study how Scouting is set out therein. You will notice in the first place that the book is divided up into Camp Fire Yarns, an indication of the method that the Chief himself followed at the first Scout Camp. These are not lectures or talks, but yarns ; not just plain yarns, but yarns told round the camp fire while the logs smoulder and the flames flit across faces and a happy, companionable warmth is induced. A camp fire immediately conveys the idea of the open air, of happiness and of companionship ; there is also something adventurous in it. So it is that by this simple division the Chief indicates to you the way you should set about things.

Study further and you will soon realise that when the Chief wanted to push any idea home he made use of a tale or anecdote and then indicated a practice. In this way the different facts of Scouting are illustrated, and then those listening to the yarn are told to see what they themselves can do in that direction.

In some similiar fashion it should be the endeavour of eve Scouter to make the work of the Troop an adventure, to weave round it some kind of a romantic setting. The way in which this is done must, of course, depend on individual taste, but no one is so prosaic that he cannot introduce something that is unexpected, that he cannot weave some kind of story round an otherwise dry Scout practice. Much of Scouting is adventurous and romantic in itself, camping and the most of our open-air work. That is one of the reasons why it is so important to keep the OUT in Scouting. There are generally two ways of doing things, one of which is wrong. For instance, signalling can be confined to the Troop Headquarters and only used in a place where it is much easier and quicker to convey the required information by word of mouth. But as soon as you get out of doors and send a Patrol to the top of a hill, and tell them what to do by signalling to them, the exercise takes on a totally different complexion. Not only is there some use in it, but it becomes a bit exciting.

It takes a little more time for a Scouter to make up a little story as a setting to a wide game, to work out some kind of a surprise competition for a winter meeting, but the results are out of all proportion to the time spent.

There is nothing in our Scouting that cannot be enriched if we only take a little trouble.

As Ernest Raymond writes, " Your eye cannot fall on anything, be it ever so small, without it being a potential crystal in which the whole of Romance can be seen. Romance is everywhere. ' Lift the stone and you shall find me ; cleave the wood and there am I.' "

It is not only the things we do and the way we do them that matter ; an atmosphere of romance and adventure can be induced by our surroundings. This is especially so in camp, and our choice of site for a camp should be governed by that consideration. Even indoors, in our normal meeting-place, something can be done to secure an atmosphere in which Scouting—real Scouting—will thrive, but more of that anon.

The majority of us too will have some past experiences on which we can draw ; practically everything can be turned to good account in some way or other, and so I will finish with an illustration culled from an article contributed to *The Times*—" Folded Tents—Looking back on the Camp "—" He minds his tent-pegging days, too, does the Scoutmaster; and though the speed of a boy of 15, ' galloping ' as best he may beneath the weight of a boy of 12, does not give that whirlwind momentum that will lift a peg, with a mighty ' Ha ! ' clean out of the ground, still a sharpened stave for lance or sword and a whitewashed potato for peg serve the purpose tolerably well ; and on sports day, when the parents come over with picnic baskets for themselves and tuck for their sons, the Troop show t em, in their gymkhana, Ranelagh isn't the only place.''

PAMPHLETS.
*Discipline in the Scout Movement.* I.H.Q., 2d.
*Tracking Rules for Scouters.* I.H.Q., 2d.

BOOKS.

ˈScouting Sketches, Hampton. Pearson, 3s. 6d. (Illustrates the way in which romance enriches Scouting.)
Good Scouting, Vera Barclay. Sheed and Ward, 3s. 6d. (Especially Chap. IX on " Scout Discipline.")

## CHAPTER VII

### ASSISTANCE IN BUILDING

IT is a great mistake to start off on the assumption that you can do everything in Scouting for yourself. It is quite obvious that every one of us is the better for help, whether it is of an active nature or more passive and takes the form of good wishes and encouragement. It is quite clear that we need our own domestic staff of Assistant Scoutmasters and Patrol Leaders. We should, however, look for, and can expect, help from others as well. Rome was not built in a day, neither was it built by one person. A really good Scout Troop cannot be built in a day, and, although it may be possible, it is certainly not advisable, that there should be only one builder.

*Parents*

Obviously the first people whose assistance we require, and whose co-operation is essential to sucess, are the parents of the boys who are, or intend to be, Scouts. In the first instance they help in producing the boys with whom we play the Game of Scouting. We owe them consideration on that account alone. There are many Scouters, however, who seem to regard parents as a race apart, even as strange specimens that ought to be within a zoological garden. Such Scouters do not quite appreciate the fact that the parents of their Scouts may have somewhat similar opinions of them. Others of us adopt a patronising attitude which gives the impression that we know all about the upbringing of boys, that parents are a necessary nuisance and are to be suffered as such, but that they know nothing of their boys and are not capable of looking after them.

Such attitudes are all wrong, and will do infinite harm to individual Scouts and to the Troop as a whole. The average parent knows quite as much as we about his boy and his upbringing, and is quite as anxious that he should turn out a decent fellow. The average parent, when he understands what Scouting really stands for, is quite prepared to take an interest in and encourage his son's Scout activities. This is true of Mothers as well as of Fathers—more so perhaps in some walks of life.

It is, therefore, very important, as has already been indicated, that the Scoutmaster should make every endeavour to get into personal touch with the parents of his Scouts, and to see that they understand what Scouting is aiming at through his endeavours. Personal visits to the boys' homes are always recommended, and are worth the extra trouble involved. Instead of an abstract " He," the Scouter becomes a personality that the boy's family can recognise, and, we hope, appreciate. The Scouter will also gain some kind of an insight into the boy's home life and conditions that may be of value to him in coming to a correct estimate of his character, and in laying down the tentative lines along which he proposes to work for its development.

Parents in their turn should be invited to pay a visit from time to time to the Scout Troop. A special invitation should be extended to them to be present at the Investiture of their own boys ; it is wise to get the boys concerned to concur in the invitation first of all. A more general invitation can be extended to them to drop in on Troop nights, but it is usually best to set aside special Parents' Evenings. On such occasions the normal activities of the Troop should be carried on as if there were no spectators present. Special Displays or Socials can also be arranged when rather a fuss is made of the visitors ; a short report of the Troop's progress is perhaps given ; the Commissioner or some other notability is asked to meet them. Similarly, if the Troop is not camping too far afield, a Visitors' Day can be appointed in camp, when the Troop's guests can be entertained in any way thought suitable.

So far we have been concerned with the steps to be taken by the Scouter to secure interest without any definite return. We must realise, however, that the mere interest of parents is a very real help to our Scouting ; the interest they show in the Troop and in their own boys' Scouting will inevitably have an influence on the boys' Scout activities. Yet there are definite ways in which we can secure the active help of parents. Many Troops have secured the assistance of parents on the Scout Group Committee. Some Troops have separate Parents' Committees ; some have a Ladies' Committee. In such cases it soon becomes evident that the happy family of the Troop spreads from the boys to their parents, and there are cases on record where the whole well-being of a community has been influenced. I could cite cases in London and in Australia—to mention no others—where the Scout Troop is the active centre of the life of the community.

One of the best means of securing a person's interest is to give him something to do. Apart from membership of committees, it is possible to get parents—as well as others—to do odd jobs in connection with the Troop. A father can help with transport, or with an odd job of carpentry ; a mother can help by preparing tea for a special meeting, or by sewing curtains or cloths. Some can act as instructors in different Scout subjects. A mother can, and often does, instruct in cooking, ambulance, or health. A father can give special instruction in signalling, carpentry, handyman, or in numerous of the trade badges.

I have devoted a considerable amount of space to this question of parents, but I have by no means exhausted the possibilities of the help they can give. I believe that there is a real need in Scouting to make a point of securing the co-operation and active assistance of the parents of Scouts from their first essay in Scouting until they have reached man's estate. By so doing we will help our Scouts and will further their Scouting, and will also widen the scope of our influence.

## The Church

I make use of the term church to include all forms of religion, whether Established or not. I am not going into the question of Scouting's religious policy now ; that deserves a chapter to itself. It is a question of the help that we may expect to obtain from pastors with which we are immediately concerned.

If a new Troop is being started in any locality it is advisable to consult the various Padres of the locality, both for advice and for information. They are aware of the needs of the locality so far as any form of social service is concerned. Their help can be a real advantage to us. Their opposition, even if just passive, is very difficult to make way against. There are some who oppose Scouting, because no one has taken the trouble to explain Scouting to them, or because some individual Scouter has failed in the past, and they have been unable to appreciate the fact that the failure of the personal element should not be allowed to entail the condemnation of the Scout method. Mention has been made of the question of controlled Church Groups. If a Troop is started definitely in connection with a Church or Chapel, then the Scouter has to realise his obligations towards the Padre. If an open Troop is started then the Scouter has to be equally careful to see that he does not offend the representatives of any existing religious body in the neighbourhood. Sometimes we hear complaints of opposition from the Church which are the direct outcome of lack of thought and consideration on the part of the Scouters concerned.

Padres can help us immensely by their encouragement, by a timely word in season to the congregation or individual members thereof, by allowing us the use of church halls, by acting as Chaplains. Many of them—of all denominations—are amongst the best Scouters we have ; others are not so good : but the lay Scouter varies much more in his quality from the real Scout point of view.

## The School

There is another body which is intensely interested in the question of the development of boys, and that is the teaching profession. Public, Preparatory and other Secondary Schools are entitled to have controlled Groups according to Rule 2, and these controlled Groups are governed by Rule 80 in certain particulars.

All open Groups, however, contain boys who are of school age, and so the importance of being in agreement with teachers appears to be obvious.

These men and women are dealing with the same boys as we are. Despite the handicaps under which many of them labour as regards overwork and numbers, they have considerable knowledge of the individual boys and of their characters, and it will be of enormous help to us if we are allowed to compare notes. First of all we have to realise that Scouting is subsidiary to the ordinary education that the boy receives ; it is an additional aid to his development. The Chief Scout never intended that Scouting should in any way take the place of the education provided by the State, local authority, or private enterprise. Having grasped this truth, we have to see that we respect it. There have been faults on both sides as regards petty quarrels and jealousies between Scouting and Schooling in the past, but the blame lies with the Scouters, for it was their duty to give way.

Now there has been a distinct change in the attitude of one to another, and it is generally realised that Scouting and Schooling can dovetail into each other for the benefit of the boy. The duty of every Scoutmaster is to see to it that this is the case as regards his Troop.

Some educational authorities now include certain Badge subjects in Evening Schools ; some allow attendance at a Troop meeting as counting for evening classes ; some allow attendance at properly organised Rallies to count as school attendance and grant leave accordingly.

In country districts the Padre and the Schoolmaster should be the Scouter's chief allies.

### Other Helpers

There is not space enough to indicate all the different kind of people who can assist us with our building operations. Anyone who can lend a hand will prove himself useful. The Doctor can give talks on ambulance work, instruct and examine for the Ambulance Man and Public Health Man Badges, give talks to the older fellows on the Tenth Scout Law, advise us in regard to precautions to be taken in camp and otherwise, generally and in individual cases. The Banker can help with the Finance of the Troop, act as Treasurer, give talks on thrift and other matters. The Grocer can advise us in regard to the ordering of stores for camp, and will frequently provide goods at special rates. Policemen can give us advice and not a few hints which will come in useful in our Scouting; they have realised that Scouting can help towards law and good order, just as their first important duty now is prevention, not detection. Employers can find employment for Scouts in preference to boys who are untrained in Scout principles and methods. Landed proprietors can furnish camp sites, and allow Scouts access to parks and woods for outdoor work.

I have met Scouters who complained that no one took any interest in their work ; in most cases the reason was that the Scouters made no attempt to interest them. Interest must be invited first before it will step in.

### The Public

First then we should try to interest as many as we can and get them to understand what we are driving at. Afterwards it will be necessary to show them how they can help in the right way. Secure some kind of an understanding ; secure the right kind of help from the right kind of people, help that is neither charity nor patronage. Do not neglect the public. Induce them to come to meetings, rallies and committees. Get them to come and talk to the Troop ; many can give interesting talks on all kinds of subjects and are glad to do so. Beware, however, of the would-be public speaker, and of those who " orate." Educate people in prominent positions to look as a matter of course to the Scouts for help, so long as the work expected of them does not interfere with the work that should be done by paid men. Induce your Scouts to put their striving after unselfishness into actual operation in the practice of good turns.

If you can arouse the interest of the public—and it is not a very difficult thing to do—you will find that anyone can be of real use and will help to keep Scouting on the move, but be particularly careful to see that the Scouting your Troop does gives them full value for their interest. Scouting is now an accepted factor in the life of the community, and we have to keep a careful guard continually to see that it remains an influence for good.

PAMPHLET.
*Scouting and Education.* I.H.Q., 2d.

BOOK.
*School Scout Troops*, Reynolds. Pearson, 2s.


## CHAPTER VIII

### LAYING THE FIRST COURSES

Now that we have laid our foundations, collected some materials, and secured a certain amount of assistance, it is possible for us to start the work of erecting our building. This must be done brick by brick, course by course, as we have already learned. A far too common mistake both in new Troops and in long-standing Troops is to rush a boy too quickly through his Scouting so that he has no real opportunity of grasping and retaining what he is taught. Every Scouter would do well to reflect on a very wise remark of

R. L. Stevenson : " It is good to have been young in youth, and as years go on to grow older. Many are already old before they are through their teens, but to travel deliberately through one's ages is to get the heart out of a liberal education." We do want our boys to realise the heart of Scouting, and so every advance we make should be well planned and carefully executed, and at each stage in our advance we should halt and consolidate our position thoroughly before going on to attack the next stage.

### The Tenderfoot Tests

Rule 26 reads : " To become a Scout, a boy must be between the ages of 11 and 18. He can remain a Scout up to any age.

" He must satisfy his Scoutmaster that he knows the Scout Law, signs and salute ; the composition of the Union Jack and the right way to fly it ; the uses of the Scout staff ; the following knots—reef, sheet bend, clove-hitch, bowline, fisherman's, sheepshank—and understand their special uses ; and how to whip the end of a rope."

The normal boy cannot secure knowledge of all these particulars in a day or a week, yet I have known a Scoutmaster satisfied with what a boy knew after a single hour's preparation. Fortunately or unfortunately, as the case may be, when I saw the boy some months later he knew nothing of his Tenderfoot tests. This kind of thing is not fair to the boy himself. He has nothing on which to build his Scouting. He is no Scout, but what is more important, a Scoutmaster like that is no Scout either.

It is worth while then paying particular attention to these tests and seeing that the boy understands them thoroughly, so thoroughly that he has not much chance of being able to forget any of them throughout the rest of his Scouting. It is to be remembered that first impressions are all-important, and that the way in which the boy learns and does his Scouting at the very beginning of his Scout life—in fact before his Scout life actually begins—will influence and colour the whole of his Scouting thereafter. Easy come, easy go. That which is difficult to attain to is worth winning, and that is the attitude of mind of the normal boy.

Attention has already been paid to the Scout Law, but I should like to lay emphasis again on one or two points. Remember that the Scout Law can be accepted as a natural code by the boy, and that he can understand it because of the way it is expressed. Refrain, therefore, from any kind of a grown-up explanation. Leave most of the teaching to the boy's future Patrol Leader or to the Scout who is training him in the hopes of gaining his First-class Badge. When satisfying yourself that the boy knows the Law, do not be content with a parrot-like repetition of its wording. Try and ascertain if the boy has grasped some of the meaning that lies behind the words. It may be possible to ask him to act, or give incidents in illustration of, one or two of the Laws ; sometimes it is easier for a boy to depict the meaning he sees in actions rather than words. Lay emphasis on the fact that these are the qualities which he should try and bring into his ordinary everyday life at home and at school, as well as in the Troop. Let him realise that as his Scoutmaster you are going to trust him to do this on his own, and are not going to be asking him questions about it. You are not going to cheapen the Law by constantly saying " A Scout does not . . ." in petty matters. Now and then after he has become a Scout you will have a chat with him in case he needs help.

Above all, keep a sense of proportion yourself, and try and get him to appreciate the fact that the whole of his Scouting depends upon the Scout Law.

The Scout signs which the boy has to learn are easy, but his knowledge should be more than just an understanding of the patterns required. A Scout takes the lead and makes signs on the ground, or elsewhere, in order that those following after him can tell where he has gone, or even receive information that he wants to convey to them. The Tenderfoot signs are just the beginnings of a code of signals that are full of interest and fun. He is a poor Scout who does not add more to his list, so that he can be of the fullest use to anyone who follows along his trail. An important feature in the test should be the making of the signs on the ground, not on the blackboard, or on a piece of paper. Encourage the use of natural materials for the making of the signs, and aim at a certain degree of efficiency so that the signs, while being apparent to Scouts, are not necessarily apparent to anyone who passes by that way. Camp Fire Yarn No. 4 and *Letters to a Patrol Leader* contain all the information that it is necessary to know.

Try and treat the Salute and the Union Jack tests in some similar way, so that not only has the boy the necessary knowledge but also some idea of what these tests mean and why he is asked to do them. One might add that it is up to the Scouters to be particularly careful in the rendering of the Scout Salute, and to see that all their boys know how to give it when carrying a Staff. *Scouting for Boys* and Roland Philipps' book give all the necessary information. It is not my object to repeat what is already available, but more to draw attention to values and needs.

We need not worry much about the uses of the Staff, except to say that it is an essential part of the Scout's uniform, and one on which the Chief Scout is particularly keen. There is romance and adventure in it provided every boy has his own and is encouraged to decorate it and look on it as his Scout totem. Apart from its uses the boy should have a knowledge of how to carry it. This will entail a certain amount of practice, but a certain amount of drilling is necessary in every Troop to ensure that the Scouts are smart and can move properly so that they are not a discredit to Scouting when they appear in public. There is no need to let any practice in drill extend beyond ten minutes at a time, nor

need it be a dull affair if it is of the silent variety when signals
are given instead of words of command, if the movements are
carried out with great rapidity, or if games such as " O'Grady
says " are employed. Five minutes' silent or rapid drill is a very
useful warmer on a cold winter's evening.

So far as knotting and whipping are concerned there is another
book—*Knotting*—which can be used in addition to the two already
mentioned. Here again try and see that the uses of the knot are
properly appreciated, and that some kind of a habit has been acquired. Knowledge of a knot implies the ability to tie it under
almost any circumstances, and not only that, but the ability to tie
the right knot in the right place.

It is important in all our Scout practices that we should make
use of real things as far as possible. Real cordage should be used
for knots ; not only is there the question of the knot, but of the
type of rope that should be selected for the knot. For instance,
if a boy is asked to demonstrate what knot he would use to save
a person from drowning, it is not the slightest bit of good tying
a bowline at the end of a small piece of twine ; he should search
for the right type and length of line first of all, coil it, tie his bowline, and be ready to throw the bowline end of it. The more all
these tests and the practice for them can be acted the better, but
be careful to avoid the danger of acting them always in the same
way.

When a boy has satisfied his Scoutmaster in regard to all these
tests he has qualified himself for admission to the Scout Brotherhood and is permitted to take the Scout Promise. If, however,
he has been a Wolf Cub, he is already a member of the Brotherhood, but that does not absolve him from the necessity of qualifying
as a Tenderfoot Scout. It is most desirable that the preparation
for the tests should be done with the Troop and not with the
Pack. The Cub should be trained by his future Patrol Leader
or another Scout just in the same way as any other boy. He will
have had the advantage of knowing something about the flag and
the knots already, and should be expected to acquire the necessary
knowledge and ability in a shorter time, and to show a higher
standard. If his Tenderfoot training is done in the Pack there is
a real danger of poaching on Scout preserves, while the Cub himself does not get any opportunity of realising that the Scout atmosphere is different and its methods not quite the same. Frequently both Cubmaster and Scoutmasters make the mistake of
doing away with the Cub-Scout's apprenticeship in the Troop. It
can be shortened, but it should not be abolished.

### The Scout Investiture Ceremony

It is of extreme importance that every endeavour should be made
to give a boy a fit and proper start along the Scout road. A great
deal of his further progress depends on the introduction he gets

to Scouting. If his investiture has made an impression on him, he will carry that impression with him throughout his journey, and it will be of immense help and strength to him. The main lines of the ceremony are set out on page 42 of *Scouting for Boys* (1929), and these lines should be carefully followed. The night before, say, the Scoutmaster should see the boy—whom he has previously tested—and run over the main features of the ceremony with him, so that he understands not only what he has to say but also what he has to do. There is an opportunity here for a short chat on the Law and Promise and all that they imply. This will serve as the rehearsal of the ceremony so far as the two chief participants in it are concerned.

Other preparations include the choice of time and place, the number of boys to be invested, the immediate preparations by the Troop as a whole. Most of these depend on circumstances. If a new Troop is being started, the two or three Patrol Leaders should be the first to be invested. It is always a mistake to invest more than two or three at a time, because either the chorus effect destroys the real personal equation, or the repetition produces boredom. Troop Headquarters, the Church, the open air are all places where investiture can be held according to the nature of the Troop. Sometimes they are held at ordinary meetings, sometimes at special meetings. In any case avoid making a public display of what should be an intimate family ceremony. If an investiture is held at an ordinary meeting, I have a preference personally for it being done early on in the proceedings. A short yarn afterwards will enable the Scouts to adjust themselves to more ordinary proceedings. If a boy has to wait till the end of a meeting he is apt to get more and more nervous as time goes on, while the ceremony itself may be scamped and hurried and affected adversely by a " want to get away " feeling.

One very important point is that the correct person to administer the Promise is the Scoutmaster himself. He is in personal contact with the boy, is known to him, and is the guardian of the Troop's honour. His very presence thereafter is frequently a source of strength to the boy who is having rather a hard time of it. If we want to interest or honour others, we can ask them to attend, and, possibly, to give a short yarn. The real Scout Commissioner understands this. But, if the Scoutmaster is to administer the Promise, he should already have taken it himself. This can be done by the Commissioner, or failing him by another Scouter, either in the presence of the boys or otherwise. If it is a new Troop this affords the Scoutmaster an opportunity to give the lead to his future Scouts.

Some thought and care should be given to see that the proper atmosphere for the ceremony is created. This is to a certain extent a matter of time and place, but can always be greatly helped by a short yarn told with the intention of attuning the minds of all those present to the inner significance of what is taking place.

When the atmosphere is created then the Troop should be drawn up in horseshoe formation as quickly and as quietly as possible. This should be done by an Assistant Scoutmaster or by a Patrol Leader, the Scoutmaster and the Recruit standing aside till all is ready. The Recruit can then be stationed in his proper place and the Scoutmaster told that all is ready.

Before commencing the ceremony I would strongly advise the Scoutmaster to say just a few words of appeal to the Troop as a whole, reminding them of the time that they took their Promise and laying stress on the importance of the words " to do my best." The ceremony can then proceed, introducing one or two minor local touches if desired, but taking care to ensure that the giving of the Promise remains the climax. Shortness and simplicity will achieve the solemnity that we should all strive for. Despite the solemnity, however, the note struck at the end should be one of joy and congratulation and welcome, and a cheer or yell for the new Scout can easily achieve this.

Once he has made his Promise the boy becomes a Tenderfoot Scout and, but not till then, is entitled to wear a Scout badge and distinctive Scout uniform.

BOOK.

*Knotting*, " Gilcraft." Pearson, 1s. 6d. and 2s. 6d.


CHAPTER IX

WORKING TO PLAN

ONCE the Tenderfoot stage has been passed, not only does the boy come into his own as a Scout, but the Patrol and the Troop also come to life actively.

From the very beginning it is necessary to introduce some kind of method into our work. Primarily it is the Scoutmaster's job to insure this ; later on as progress is made it will become the function of the Court of Honour, that is, the corporate body of Scouters and Patrol Leaders.

What we should do all the time is to keep in our minds the Chief's definition of Scouting as " the work and attributes of back-woodsmen, explorers and frontiersmen." This entails at least an out-of-door atmosphere in our work. The vagaries of our climate are such that perforce a great deal of our Scout work has to be done indoors, but that is not a sufficient excuse for staying indoors always. We should make a point of getting out whenever it is at all possible. This is not so difficult as one imagines provided one is prepared with alternative programmes winter and summer, provided one instils the tradition in the Troop that " we do our Scouting outside, and only come in when we have to." The same applies whether the Troop is a town one or is in a country district. The original Boy Scouts did not gather together in clubrooms ; the streets and the fields and the woods were their clubrooms.

As I have said we have to do a great deal of our work indoors, but even then we should give the out-of-doors a prominent place, and our activities should be directed in the main to preparing for outdoor Scouting, so that we do not waste time when we are out. Clubrooms are good things in their way, and boys' clubs do a lot of good work, but they are not Scouting.

Largely it is a matter of getting the right atmosphere, helped perhaps by some small scheme of decoration, but it is the activities themselves and the way in which they are presented that are of supreme importance.

### Indoor Programmes

It is a good plan to settle on some general scheme of activities for a period of, say, three months. In drawing up that scheme the Court of Honour should search out for the Troop's weak spots first of all with a view to strengthening them, then they can select any particular activity or activities that individual Patrols or the Troop as a whole can take up. It is a very good plan to have some central idea running through the scheme as providing a backbone to the skeleton and as giving an opportunity to mark the advance that the Patrol or the Troop as a whole is making.

With a new Troop things are fairly easy, because work for the Second-class tests can be the backbone round which the programme is built. Afterwards it becomes more difficult, the older Scouts want to progress, the younger ones have to be practised in more elementary Scouting. But the revision the older Scouts need and the practice the younger Scouts want can very easily be allied from time to time. Individual progress is a matter for the individual Scout, and that truism needs appreciating.

There should be at least one Troop night on a fixed day and at a fixed time every week. If possible other nights of the week should be devoted to Patrol meetings—in which the majority of the practices for tests should be done, to special gatherings for badge work, singing, country dancing and the like.

So far as the Troop night is considered the Scoutmaster is primarily and ultimately responsible, with the advice of his Court of Honour, for its conduct. It is best for him to draw up his skeleton programme, discuss it with his Assistants and Patrol Leaders and work out the details for himself. In working out details he should bear in mind that he has to satisfy the normal boy, not just those who are keen and eager. To satisfy him he will have to provide a sufficiency of interest, variety and activity. The normal boy enjoys games, and games must be provided, but varying in their nature and devised to make for all-round development—not just physical development ; his body, his brains, his nerves, his Scouting qualities all call for development. The normal boy also enjoys work, provided that work is presented to him in an attractive form and is full of interest. The work may be new, when its freshness will attract and stimulate him to endeavour. The work may be old, and will encourage him to try out his skill if it is presented to him in somewhat of a new way.

It is a good thing from time to time for the Scoutmaster to be a spectator for the whole meeting, leaving its control and conduct to his Assistants or to the Troop Leader. It is certainly good training for them.

It would destroy initiative and individuality to lay down a series of programmes for each Scoutmaster to follow. Apart from that there cannot be any ideal series of programmes. Our Troop work is governed by the needs and stages of the boys in our Troop and not by any eclectic considerations.

The Scouter can obtain help from *How to Run a Troop*, but he will probably find that the programmes detailed there need more time than is allowed. He can find more details in Chapter V of *School Scout Troops* and in other books.

Punctuality, cleanliness, uniform, having gear ready, the Duty Patrol, are all in a sense minor—although not unimportant—considerations. The main point is that the programme we offer is sufficient to attract the boy even if he is just a mediocre Scout, to give him something he wants, to satisfy his urge to be up and doing. If it is not sufficiently attractive the pictures may win ; it is not for us to blame the pictures, but ourselves. A challenge has been thrown down and we must accept it. It is not fair to the boy to expect him to turn up to meetings because he is a Scout ; there must be other reasons than that to induce him to come.

All this will entail considerable thought, considerable preparation, considerable study of boys and books, considerable talk with other Scouters, considerable determination. It is not enough to scrape through. We must win hands down.

Unexpectedness helps ; apart from Scouters and Patrol Leaders there is no need to advertise programmes ; the order in which things are done can be varied ; the normal practice can go by the board altogether ; surprise items can be introduced ; competitions can be varied ; Patrol Leaders can take charge of the evening. There are five varieties in as many lines.

There are other points worthy of special mention.

If Patrols do not meet separately, and it is highly desirable that they should, see that a period of some twenty minutes is set aside for Patrol work at Troop meetings. Sometimes it is advisable that the Court of Honour should indicate what should be done in this period, but it is best to leave it to the Patrol Leaders themselves to decide what they will do and how they will do it. Latitude in this respect is good for them, and gets them to see that they are responsible for the well-being of their Patrols. If they ask for help, it should be given, but only on special occasions. During this time the Scouters have an opportunity of going about and seeing how the Patrol Leaders are setting about their job, and whether they are bringing the individual members of their Patrols on.

Remember the materials that are available to our hands in our building, and do not forget that *Scouting for Boys* is built up on camp-fire yarns. Both yarns and camp fires, even indoors, can be turned to good account. The yarn by one of the Scouters, or by someone else, whether instructional or otherwise, should be one of the features of the meeting. It is possible even to use the original camp-fire yarns in order to teach Scouting !

In every programme some kind of a balance should be maintained between active and passive, demonstration and initiative, work and games, Troop and Patrol. It will be found that normally twenty minutes is quite long enough for any one item. It is just as important that the meeting should close punctually as that it should open punctually, in order that the Scouts may get home at a regular hour. Some kind of ceremonial, including a simple prayer, if possible, should be observed at the close of the meeting in the same way as the Union Flag is broken at the commencement.

### Competitions

Many, in these modern days, decry all competition and stigmatise it as non-moral. Then the whole of nature is non-moral, for it is competition that produces all that grows. Whatever the theories on the matter may be, however, there is no doubt about the practicability of it.

The normal boy is a natural animal, for which we may be thankful, and instinctively tries to pit his mind and strength against others. Personally I hold that that instinct is not a wrong one. Competition is a spur and incentive, a challenge to the individual to put his best foot forward instead of lazily watching the rest go by. It is much better that this instinct should be developed along right lines and gradually trained into a team spirit, than that it should remain merely a selfish urge or degenerate into a desire to do the other fellow down. Apart from everything else inter-Patrol competitions have a value in character training. The individual is asked to develop himself in order that his Patrol may benefit : Patrol struggles in friendly, healthy rivalry against Patrol in order that the Troop may benefit.

The average Scouter can, and should, make use of the competitive element in order to encourage, revise and test the training in various Scout practices that the Patrols are receiving. By these means he will find where the weak spots lie and will be able to take steps to strengthen them. The Scouter must, however, be particularly careful to note any signs of unhealthy rivalry creeping in, of any idea being entertained that it is the Patrol or Troop that

matters as against Scouting as a whole. He must take care that
competitions are not overdone, so that the Game of Scouting is
lost sight of, and, in consequence, extreme efficiency in one or
two subjects regarded as of more importance than the development
of the boys' characters.

As with games and programmes and everything else considerable
variety should be introduced into competitions so that they range
throughout the whole of the Scouting that the Troop is taking
up, and suit the conditions of each Scout and each Patrol in
turn.

As a rule the Court of Honour should draw up any inter-Patrol
competitions on a three-monthly, or even monthly, basis. A long-
drawn-out competition is a mistake and usually defeats its own
object. From time to time surprise items can be introduced devised by the Scouters without the previous knowledge of the Patrol
Leaders.

Sometimes the subject of next week's special inter-Patrol competition can be announced, if it is a general weakness ; this gives
the Patrols an opportunity to rub up their knowledge in that subject throughout the week.

There is no need here to say much on the subject of Association
and District Competitions. They have a value if they are so devised
that they stimulate real Scouting, but there is great difficulty in
devising conditions fair to the very varying circumstances of different Troops. They have a danger if they cause dissensions between
Troops or petty jealousies between Scouters. In any case they do
not come within the scope of this book.

Competitions as a whole, however, are intimately connected with
the making up of Troop programmes, whether indoor or outdoor,
but more especially the former. They are effective as adding the
necessary spice which will make the Scouts who are perhaps not
so keen as the others strive a bit harder than they otherwise would.
The manner in which they are conducted varies considerably, and
many suggestions will be found in *The Scouter* from time to time.
The honour of being on top is usually sufficient compensation for
the leading Patrol. If any actual trophy seems desirable, see that it
is something that has no intrinsic value. The reward lies in the
knowledge that a certain amount of progress has been made, and
every Patrol in the Troop can sense something of that reward.
The Scoutmaster's attention should be directed towards the lowest
Patrol. Is it below the others because the Troop programmes do
not suit it or because the Patrol Leader is weak ? He should not
judge his Troop by the best Patrol, but by the worst which requires
the most help.

## BOOKS.

*How to Run a Troop*, Young. Pearson, 1s. 6d. and 2s. 6d.

*The Scout Way*, Vera Barclay. Sheed and Ward, 2s. 6d. (Part
II, Chap. I, Competitions and Programmes.)

D

## CHAPTER X

### ADDING ANOTHER STOREY

WHEN a boy has been invested as a Scout he is then able to go on
to the next grade, that of Second-class Scout. It is for Patrol
Leaders and Scouters to see that this stage is definitely tackled by
each Scout. A certain amount of encouragement is needed, but
the Tenderfoot Scout will be quite eager to go on provided he is
given opportunities of practice in the Second-class tests; work in
connection with them is incorporated in Troop programmes, and
the road is pointed out to him without delay. It is not right that
a boy should do any intensive Second-class work before he is invested; but he should be allowed to come with the others and
have some practice shots so that his keenness may be stimulated.
It is equally not right that there should be any delay in putting
him on to definite Second-class work as soon as he has actually
become a Scout.

The question " What are we to do with our Scouts ? " can frequently be easily solved by " Push along with their Second-class
and First-class tests." Even with Scouts at different stages of development it is possible to arrange programmes that will suit all.
In inter-Patrol competitions it is possible to devise conditions that
will give equal chances to all Scouts. In surprise competitions it
is possible to devise events so that those working for Second-
class in a Patrol do one thing, and those working for First-class do
another.

The actual conditions that a Tenderfoot Scout must satisfy in
order to win the Second-class Badge are set out in *Policy, Organisation and Rules*. It would take up more space than I can spare
to reproduce them here, but I will touch upon one or two of the
more salient features.

To begin with the Badge is awarded on the recommendation of
the Scoutmaster, which authorises him to arrange for the tests
being taken either by himself or his Assistant Scoutmasters. This
authorisation carries with it the obligation to assure himself that
the Scouts he recommends are really worth their salt. The tests
are not difficult ones, and it is important that the Scouters of the
Troop should themselves be able to do them. This is not too
much to expect and should be a point of honour with all Scouters.
Inability to accomplish any of the simple Tenderfoot and Second-
class tests will depreciate their stock, so to speak, amongst their
Scouts. Scouting as a whole comprises so many subjects that it
is impossible for any one man to expect to know them all. No
man or boy expects that, but the Scouts can legitimately expect
us to know the simple tests ourselves. How otherwise can we
teach, or check the teaching of them ?

### Service

A minimum of one month's service as a Tenderfoot is laid down as essential. This service starts from the date of the Scout's investiture, not from the date of his passing his Tenderfoot tests. This is one reason why a boy's investiture should not be unduly delayed. The one month is very much of a minimum ; normally one would not expect a boy to pass his Second-class tests properly under a period of three months, and even that is short. Service *as* a Tenderfoot also implies that the boy continues to possess the knowledge and ability required by the Tenderfoot tests and that he is doing his best to live up to the ideals of the Scout Law. The Scoutmaster should assure himself on this point before he makes his final recommendation. If all our Scouters would only realise that boys like to have things done thoroughly, and appreciate the reasons for it, our Scouting would be a much better thing. Too often the boys' standards are lowered by the slackness of their Scouters.

### First-Aid

The knowledge and ability required of a Second-class Scout in respect of first-aid are quite definite. He must have a knowledge of the general rules of health as given in Camp-Fire Yarns 17, 18 and 19. He must be able to deal with certain specified simple accidents. He must know how to clean a wound and apply a dressing. He must know how to apply a triangular bandage to different parts of the body, but is not asked to have anything to do with fractures.

Apart from hearing about the general rules of health he should be given an opportunity of reading them up for himself. It is best to lend him a copy of *Scouting for Boys* for this purpose ; perhaps he may read other portions of it and benefit accordingly. Don't dish him out with a précis or with a pamphlet on the subject ; let him go straight to the original. Otherwise our teaching in regard to the first-aid tests should be very simple, very definite and very practical. There is no need for the boy to study other books ; in fact practically all that he needs to know even in regard to health is contained on page 32 of *Scouting for Boys*.

The training should be spread over several weeks and arranged as short talks and longer practices. A great deal, if not all, of it can be done by Patrol Leaders or First-class Scouts—it is a good thing to give the First-class Scouts who are not Patrol Leaders opportunities of leadership. The Scoutmaster should, however, come to a decision as to the best method to use in all cases, and should see that that method, and not various alternatives which may confuse, is taught. The method employed should be practical from beginning to end. For instance, if it is a question of the treatment of a cut, a patient should be provided—an application of red ink will give sufficient realism. The Scout should not

then say what he thinks ought to be done, but should set about
and do it without wasting time and words.  He should find the
bottle of whatever antiseptic is favoured, obtain water, dilute the
antiseptic to the required amount and wash the " wound." Thereafter, after washing his hands, he should find the appropriate dressing, cut a piece off, place it on the " wound," cover it up and bandage it in the approved fashion.  If a sling appears necessary, it
should be made and applied.  In this way he learns how to do the
test in a practical way, and this is the method which should be
used to test him eventually.

Competitions are useful in practice, but see that emphasis is
laid on the right things.  An inter-Patrol competition in bandaging
should not be judged on time, but on neatness, accuracy, and the
ability of the bandage to stay where it is put.  A " patient " with
a bandaged knee should be asked to walk about, even to run, to
ensure that the bandage is firm.

### Signalling

Here again it is a matter of arousing the boy's interest.  Semaphore is easiest to learn, and easiest to remember, and in ordinary
Scouting practices out-of-doors is possibly of more practical value,
but then I must confess that I am not a signaller.  The normal
citizen will be well qualified with a knowledge of Semaphore, for
real signalling later on Morse is necessary.  It is a question of
making one's own decision, after the Scout concerned has had his
say, because after all he should be given some consideration.

In either case once a certain number of letters have been learnt
games and competitions can be introduced.  Avoid making signalling practice a matter of drill.  Avoid asking a Scout to signal
to another two paces away.  It is impossible in that way to convey
the idea of it all, so get out of doors as soon as possible and send
real messages, or, as one keen signaller recommends, comic remarks.

Don't ask for too much.  No speed of any kind is required for
the Second-class test, only the ability to read and send single letters
and numbers.  That is a deadly dull business if taken literally, so
liven it up by a word or two, a comic code, or anything else that
seems good to you.  At the same time get in a word or two about
the romance of it all.  The Chief Scout has given you a lead there
again.

### Tracking and Kim's Game

Having what is colloquially known as a bee in my bonnet about
both these subjects, I will try and deal very shortly with them.
To begin with, the two are not true alternatives so far as a boy's
training is concerned.  The one trains his eyes to spot things, the
other trains his brain to remember things.  If you can, and that
should not be difficult, establish a tradition in the Troop that both
are done in order to qualify for the test.  Then get hold of a copy

of Rudyard Kipling's *Kim* and read out about the training that
Kim received from Lurgan Sahib in the Simla Bazaar, and try
and outline the purpose of that training. It is well worth while
giving a considerable amount of practice in Kim's Game, starting
with quite a small number of articles, and gradually increasing
the number and reducing the time. It is of importance that a
fairly accurate description should be given of each. Introduce
variety and interest, bring in team observation. Chapter III of
*Training in Tracking* contains a number of hints that will be found
useful.

The shop-window alternative laid down is merely a variation
of Kim's Game.

The tracking test is, in a sense, a more difficult matter, and
some kind of a proper standard is harder to arrive at. Chapters
IX and X of the book mentioned deal with this quite fully. Practice is obviously required and opportunities for it should be afforded.
Here is an opportunity, if any is required, for getting outdoors.
Don't be put off by the fellow who says " It is impossible to track
in a town." He has never tried. Others have, very successfully.
Normally the trail should be made with Scout signs, using natural
materials and avoiding chalk, but there is no objection to varying
the method. The sign should be fairly closely laid and made comparatively distinct, for this is only an elementary test in tracking.
A good deal of fun and a considerable amount of exercise can be
got out of this test. Subsequently trails can be laid for the Patrols
to follow along independently at intervals of time after each other,
the last Patrol removing all traces.

*Scout's Pace*

There is only one way in which this particular test of the Scout's
Pace can be properly achieved and that is by practice under different conditions. A certain amount of application is required, and
the boy's powers of sticking to it are tried out, so that eventually
he acquires the habit of going at a certain speed for a given length
or time. It is not sufficient to have done it once with a fair degree
of accuracy, but of being able to do it any time within the same
degree of accuracy. It is not a question of two-thirds, however,
like Kim's Game ; within one-twentieth is more like the accuracy
that should be expected. The pace is a method of covering distance without fatigue that is still practised in various parts of the
world as a matter of course by various peoples. It was the Zulu
Impi that the Chief Scout had in his mind when he suggested the
test originally, and that origin enables us to appeal to the boy's
imagination. Once the test has been passed, the practice should
not be dropped. When the Troop is outdoors it is quite easy
every now and then for each Patrol to proceed at Scout's Pace
to a certain spot, to use Scout's Pace as a method of judging
the time, or of judging long distances. Observation practices

introduced from time to time on the way will again add interest.

I once had the temerity to write that the reference to Scout's Pace in *Scouting for Boys* was not very informative. Immediately the Chief sent me a note : " Zulus do forty miles a day and at good pace on it. Crawford's Light Division adopted it with good results in the Peninsula Campaign. It enables boys (and old men) to cover the ground at fairly rapid pace without strain."

### Firelighting

Here again is another opportunity of rubbing in that Scouting is an outdoor game. A fire has to be lit out of doors where wind and weather play their part. Despite the fact that a great deal of the success and enjoyment of camp depends on the ability to light a fire, very little instruction in the subject ever seems to be given. It is easy enough to light a fire on a fine calm day with plenty of dry material to hand, but the test properly applied supposes that the Scout has the ability to light a fire in all kinds of weather. So proper instruction with stress on the important maxim " start small " must be given as well as opportunities for laying and lighting fires out of doors. A certain amount of advice will be found in *Scouting Out-of-doors.*

In this apparently simple test there is scope for the learning of all kinds of things—material wherewith to start a fire, the way the material should be laid, the kinds of wood that burn well, the way the ground on which the fire is to be laid should be prepared, the way in which surrounding ground should be safeguarded, the storage of wood, the kind of fire that should be built for cooking different kinds of things, the care that should be taken to see that the fire is thoroughly out. And that does not exhaust the possibilities.

### Cooking

A start can be made indoors in regard to this test, and it should always be possible to obtain a certain amount of help at home. The indoor training is chiefly useful as emphasising cleanliness of hands and utensils and in showing how the things to be cooked should be prepared. Great attention should be paid to cleanliness, and dirty hands should at once entail failure in a test, and a post-ponement of a further test for at least a week. In affording prac-tice it has also to be remembered that cooking indoors and cooking outdoors are two different things. A wood fire is a chancy thing at times ; it requires much more care and patience. A veering wind wants watching. In fact cooking in the open shows whether the boy is really a Scout or not. So we have to see to it that some kind of a standard is insisted on.

### Saving

In this test the Scout is asked to carry out in a very small way one of the Scout Laws, just as many of the other tests he is asked to do contain something of the practical application of other Laws. Here, as everywhere in Scouting, it is the spirit that counts for most. The minimum amount to be saved would be absurd to some, while it is almost a definite hardship to others. In satisfying himself on this point the Scoutmaster has a further opportunity of seeing that the boy understands what is meant by thrift, and that he realises that he is being asked to prepare himself to be independent of others in the future.

### The Compass

" If you can keep your head when all about you
Are losing theirs and blaming it on you,

. . . . . . .

Yours is the Earth and everything that's in it,
And, which is more, you'll be a Man, my son ! "

The quotation is apposite if only a little thought is given to this very simple Second-class test. If one knows one's directions on the ground, one has more chance of keeping one's direction through life. A boy who knows his compass can keep a clear head when he is in a strange country.

So there are idealistic considerations as well as practical considerations to this and other tests.

When the Scout is being trained in compass directions, see that the training is carried out in a practical manner. It is not sufficient for him to be able to draw a compass card with all the directions nicely ruled in ; he must know directions indoors and in the open. One of the best ways of keeping everyone up to the mark in the Troop is to make a habit of giving games from time to time which involve compass directions, and to use the points of the compass, even in simple orders, instead of the words right and left.

It is an impossible matter to compress into one chapter all the lines of thought and action that are involved in the Second-class tests. I have merely tried to indicate some of these in the hope that that will be sufficient to convey what the Chief Scout intended when he first suggested these graded tests for the boy who took up Scouting. The Second-class and First-class tests can be looked upon as the framework on which the Scoutmaster should build his Scouting. Frequently they are ignored as general practices and left entirely to the individual, whereas it is expected that Scouts in general should go in for them, and their individual expressions emerge from them. We have to beware of a somewhat modern tendency to specialise at too early an age, and so we have to secure an all-round development first.

BOOKS.

*Talks on Ambulance Work,* " Gilcraft." Pearson, 1s. 6d. and 2s. 6d.
*Signalling for Scouts,* Scott and Morgan. Pearson, 1s. 6d.
*Training in Tracking,* " Gilcraft." Pearson, 5s.
*Scouting Out-of-doors,* " Gilcraft." Pearson, 1s. 6d. and 2s. 6d.

## CHAPTER XI

### ROOFING THE BUILDING

" No Scout will want to remain Second-class for longer than he need and so you will become a First-class Scout as soon as you can." So says the Chief Scout in *Scouting for Boys,* and adds : " This will mean hard work."

The First-class Badge should be the aim of every Scout, and it is within the possibilities of every Scout to attain it, if he will but try. In winning the badge a boy becomes a real Scout, not just the half-baked article. Periodical controversies range round this badge, the tests for which have remained practically the same from the time Scouting started until quite recently, when they were eased to a certain extent in order to encourage Scouters to take up the training of it. I have put it this way purposely, be-cause I believe that the small number of First-class Scouts is due to the Scouters, not to the unwillingness of Second-class Scouts to complete their Scout training. It is obviously impossible for me to take the First-class tests one by one and deal with them even as inadequately as I have dealt with the Tenderfoot and Second-class tests. What I propose to do is just to say a few words generally on the subject and to try and indicate the attitude the Scouter should adopt towards it and one or two ways by which he can secure that the majority of the boys in his Troop can set out to win the badge.

The badge as it stands at present is well within the capabilities of the average boy of fourteen to fifteen, provided he is prepared to put his back into it and make a real effort. I have already indicated that that quality is perhaps more necessary and more important to-day than it was in 1908. There are certain primary considerations which I am compelled to state somewhat shortly. To become a First-class Scout does not imply that a boy has to take a sudden plunge out of his depth all at once. He is asked to show that he can look after himself, but he is allowed to wade into it gradually. The Second-class Scout should not be expected to pass all his First-class tests at one fell swoop, but he should be expected to pass them all within a period of, say, one year from starting off to take them. This refers to the question of passing his tests, not to the question of learning or practising. It is possible and advisable to bring into the ordinary programmes of the Troop a certain amount of practice in First-class work by means of inter-Patrol competitions, games and otherwise. It is not at all necessary that any Scout should be compelled to wait until he has secured his Second-class Badge before he is allowed to obtain a little practice in the elementary parts of First-class subjects.

The actual intensive study for the various tests is a matter largely of individual effort ; opportunities for such study should be afforded, and advice and help should be given when required. It is for the Scoutmaster and the other Scouters of the Troop to do their best to encourage and help. As I have already said, the lack of First-class Badges in any Troop is usually their fault and no one else's. They will probably try and shift the blame on to the conditions, or the examiners, or the Local Association, but such excuses are very lame, as has been proved time and time again in all kinds and conditions of Troops.

Examiners and Local Associations undoubtedly have their part to play. Associations should see that an adequate panel of examiners—who understand their job—is provided, and that sufficient facilities are afforded to the boys so that they do not have to wait unnecessarily. The recent change in conditions by which Scoutmasters may be allowed to certify for half the tests laid down, will undoubtedly ease the situation so far as Scouters and Scouts are concerned. Examiners can render immense service to Scouting generally if they endeavour to help every boy who comes before them, instead of merely passing or failing him. By that I mean that when a boy fails in any particular test he should be told why he has failed and advised what he should do in order to secure the necessary knowledge or ability. If the examiner would only indicate the extra study and practice that he requires and state the period that should elapse before he has another shot, he will be helping that particular boy and helping to raise the general standard of Scouting. A certain amount of sympathy and understanding will work wonders.

And now to turn to the Scouters specially. Many of them appear to regard First-class work as something quite outside the ordinary sphere of the Troop's activities, and make no attempt to bring it into the everyday activities of the Troop. I have already said that this attitude is wrong. Many regard it as so difficult—usually without any actual personal experience, but from hearing others talk about it—that special classes are necessary for tackling the different subjects. There is nothing in the First-class test which cannot be introduced to the boy in an elementary form during the first week he is a Scout. Any Troop meeting can include competitions in estimating heights or short distances, numbers and weights, talks on mapping and axemanship, and so on. Swimming should be encouraged, observing all the precautions laid down, from a boy's earliest years without any idea of a test. What if one has to go six miles before one can find suitable water? I have known many boys—and girls—who had to walk that distance to school and back again. Even a boy of twelve can go for a short journey on a Saturday afternoon, carrying his food, and submitting some kind of a report afterwards.

When a boy has passed the Second-class stage he has merely to bring himself up to First-class standard in subjects that he should know a good deal about already. For this purpose any idea of a " special class for First-class " should be avoided, as it immediately suggests great difficulties to the Scout, which are frequently there in the imagination of the Scouter only. There is, of course, no objection to having special classes for mapping or some other special subjects, which those working specially for First-class can join, but don't confine such classes to such Scouts, they should be open to the whole Troop.

If I speak somewhat emphatically on these points it is because for the last twelve months I have taken particular care to make a special note of any First-class Scouts I met, and to question them on their experience. I have met quite a large number, and practically everyone confessed that he had found one part or other of the test rather a difficulty, but all were agreed, without being prompted, that the difficulty was worth it, and that they learned quite a lot because of it. If the Scouts themselves can adopt that attitude surely the Scouters can too.

So it is that the encouragement of the Scouter becomes such an important feature. He should talk the question of the First-class Badge over with his Court of Honour, show the members of the Court that he expects every Scout to look towards the First-class Badge as his immediate aim, discuss with them ways and means of securing opportunities for practice, arrange the Troop's programmes—indoor and outdoor—so that First-class subjects have a prominent place, establish the desire in their minds for the Troop to have the tradition of being a First-class Troop. It is quite true to say that a Troop that places the First-class Badge prominently in its programme will inevitably become a First-class Troop.

There is plenty of material to hand which will help us on the trail. *Scouting for Boys* itself is full of information about First-class work. *Letters to a Leader* is all about these tests. *Talks on Ambulance Work* goes further than is required in the test in first-aid. *Exploring* deals at length with the question of mapping and the journey.

At the risk of poaching on the preserves of the last-named book, I should like to say just a few words on the subject of the First-class journey. A First-class Scout is supposed to be one who has proved his worth, who is able to go out into the open by himself and carry out successfully any little job that is given him to do. His training has secured that he is self-reliant, self-dependent, self-assured, self-less. The journey provides the best means that

Scouting has of putting these qualities to the test. It should be the acme of the training that the Scout has received, and, as *Exploring* says, should preferably come last. My plea is that the journey should be a real test of the Scout's ability to do things on his own, and not just a Saturday afternoon's stroll. I would also add that the more practice the Scoutmaster can give by gradual degrees to the Scouts in his Troop in regard to this journey test, the more will the Scouting of the Troop progress.

A building is not habitable until it has been roofed ; a Scout is not complete until he has become First-class. It is in this direction that we want to develop our Scouting now. We should do our best to insure that every Scout really makes an attempt to become a *pucka* Scout. We do not necessary develop by increasing the scope of our Scouting so far as numbers are concerned ; real development consists in securing that all those who call themselves Scouts are Scouts in their actions and in their attitude as well as in name.

Again this applies to Scouters just as much as to Scouts.

### BOOKS.

*Letters to a Leader on the First-class Tests,* Ince. Pearson, 6d.
*Exploring,* " Gilcraft." Pearson, 1s. 6d. and 2s. 6d.

## CHAPTER XII

### DECORATING

WHEN a Scout has qualified as Second-class, not only is he allowed to go in for his First-class tests, but he can also win proficiency badges in the subjects in which he is interested.

These various badges can be placed roughly in four groups :

1. *Service Badges*—such as the badges that qualify for King's Scout, Ambulance man, Interpreter, Pathfinder and so on. The public is entitled to expect a fairly high standard of efficiency in a Scout who wears one or other of these service badges. It is essential to the good name of Scouting that that expectation should be realised, and so all King's Scout badges have to be re-qualified for every year. Scouters should pay special attention as regards the training for these badges and see that opportunities of revision are afforded.

2. *Scouting Badges*—such as Camper, Pioneer, Tracker. Training for any of these should be more of a general nature, elementary knowledge in regard to them being dealt with in ordinary Troop programmes, and revised by means of games and competitions. Once the elements of knowledge that *all* Scouts should possess of these subjects have been acquired further study can be a matter of the Scout's individual study and aptitude.

3. *Hobby Badges*—such as Airman, Bird Warden, Leatherworker, Naturalist. The object of this group of badges specially is to foster any interest which the Scout may have, so that he can fill in his leisure time usefully and happily, and so that it may be possible to lay the foundations of hobbies which will interest him throughout his life. There are other possibilities in connection with this group of badges that I will mention later.

4. *Trade Badges*—such as Blacksmith, Dairyman, Miner. The object of this group is to encourage a boy to learn his trade thoroughly and to connect it with his Scouting.

The Badge System with its training in character, hobbies, possible vocation and so on, is an integral part of the Scout method of training. It is based on a desire to draw out interest, industry and zeal, and only assist technical training incidentally. This is a somewhat important point since it is sometimes necessary to correct the attitude towards badges that has been adopted by some Scouters and Local Associations. Setting aside Service badges for the moment, the winning of a badge does not necessarily mean that the Scout is an expert in that particular line, but that he has shown a real and not a passing interest in it and has applied himself to it. The amount of interest and application will vary with the nature of the badge and the nature of the boy. Where a boy is employed in a trade and comes up for a badge in that subject it should be obvious that a good working knowledge of the subject should be expected of him. If another boy has taken up that subject as a hobby only, and his opportunities of getting acquainted with it are correspondingly limited, such a high standard of knowledge is not so necessary.

The Chief Scout has repeatedly stated his opinion in regard to badges, saying that the main object and value of them is to draw out the dull, backward boy and give him a chance with the more brilliant and better educated boy, so that the former is encouraged to make an attempt to get to know about things. He further says quite distinctly that the standard of award should not necessarily be the amount of skill or knowledge that the boy possesses, but the amount of effort that he continues to put in to his attempt. This means that there should be some kind of liaison between Scouters and Badge examiners. The latter are appointed by the Local Association, but it is always open to every Scouter to give them any information he may have as regards the boy's character and the amount of work he has put in.

Some of the uses of badges in Troop work have already been indicated. They help to form character, and certain of them are so devised as to encourage physical well-being, manual dexterity or mental concentration. They also serve as an incentive to self-help, one of the most important of Scout attributes. They are valuable also as an adjunct to winter work, and as teaching a boy something to do in his spare time, thus encouraging him to make the best use of his leisure. This is sometimes not so much a question of the present as of the future. It is an unfortunate fact that many boys, what between school-work and organised games, employment and evening classes, have no spare time of any kind. It is rather a pitiful state of affairs to my mind, because a certain amount of leisure is essential to development, and unless a man has learned how to occupy his leisure when he was young he will find it extremely difficult to do so when he is older. That is one of the reasons why ready-made pleasures are so well patronised.

The hobby group of badges help us here, and there is also a possibility through them of discovering some special aptitude in a boy which might indicate a suitable future occupation for him. Too great stress should not be laid on this point, for at the best it is only a remote possibility, but it is a point that the Scoutmaster should bear in mind and that he should address his attention to, if his watchful eyes notice any special tendency on a boy's part. These badges can only give broad indications, such, for instance, as whether the boy has greater manual skill than head skill.

The Service badges are important as carrying an obligation to the public with them. In this case some standard is necessary, as we have not only ourselves to consider. Knowledge of these subjects should be kept up to date, because at any time the service implied by the badge may have to be put into operation.

But the converse is not true, as some imagine, that there is no obligation on the Scout to retain a knowledge of other badges that he has not to be examined for annually. When a Cub is awarded a badge he makes a promise to keep on practising or trying or helping as the case may be. We may well adopt the same kind of principle in regard to all Scout badges.

There are a large number of Scout badges so that every boy may have some kind of a choice, and may find that his interests are suited in one way or another. This large number, however, suggests to some that a boy is the better Scout according to the number of badges he sports on his arm. Perhaps the All-round Cords also help to keep this impression alive. The Chief deals with this point in *What Scouts Can Do :*

" I fear that sometimes we find a fellow going in for Proficiency tests in order to get badges to wear. He likes to have a sleeve full for swank, but that fellow is not a true Scout—*he is thinking of himself* all the time.

" The true Scout is the chap who goes in for the training in order to make himself efficient and able *to help other people*. If the badge is awarded to him he is glad to have it, and proud of it, but that was not his reason for taking up the work.

" A Scout does his work because it is his duty, not for any reward. I do hope that every Scout will remember this and carry it out when he is grown up."

Badge-hogging, as it is called, can be easily avoided if the Scoutmaster will only lay emphasis on the First-class badge as the one

to aim at primarily after passing Second-class. He can perhaps
lay the trail by suggesting to the Scout or Scouts certain badges,
such as Cook, which will help towards First-class work. Later on
he can draw attention to the King's Scout badges, and then those
leading up to the Bushman's Thong, at the same time suggesting
one or two hobby badges to suit the individuality of the boy. If
some such procedure as this is followed, not only will the Scoutmaster be developing the character and abilities of his Scouts,
but he will also be developing their Scouting on to the highest
planes. In this way he will be making real use ⌐f the Badge system
in his Scouting, instead of, as sometimes happens, subordinating
his Scouting to badges.

There are certain ways and means to be considered. Sometimes it is advisable for the whole Troop or for different Patrols
in the Troop to specialise in certain badges. I would suggest that
it is best to do both. It is possible to make a selection of badges
round which the general activities of the Troop can revolve ; the
Second-class and First-class badges would obviously be so selected
and possibly others such as Camper, Healthy man, Leatherworker,
Pathfinder, Pioneer. Then each Patrol can select its own special
badges round which a certain amount of special Patrol work can
be built. If a selection of three is made, one should be drawn
from each of the Service, Scouting and Hobby groups.

Badge work should only be dealt with at Troop meetings in a
general way, but it is wonderful what an amount of knowledge
and ability the Troop as a whole can acquire in certain badge subjects, if the matter for Troop instruction is carefully chosen. It
is a mistake to bar Tenderfoots from such instruction ; they will
benefit as much as the others, although they may have to wait
longer before they can reap the reward of that benefit.

Personally I would be inclined to avoid special badge classes as
such, but there is obviously no objection to special meetings to
deal with such subjects as Carpentry, Leatherworker and so on.
What I mean is that the badge should not be the aim of these
special meetings, and they should not be so labelled ; the knowledge and ability gained is the important matter, the badge is inci-
dental, but can sometimes be used as an incentive. So again we
can say that the badge is not an end in itself but a means to an end.

### Handicrafts

Handicrafts naturally arise out of a consideration of badges, but
I am going to depart from the normal practice I have so far followed in this book, and build up the remarks I have to say on this
subject from before the Cub age, through the Pack to the Troop.

Handicrafts, or, preferably, making things, form an important
part of Scout training in a boy's life, whether he be Wolf Cub,
Scout or Rover Scout—not the most important part by any means.
The boy, before he is old enough to become a Wolf Cub, has

probably been taught how to use his fingers in some way or other in the infant class at school. When he becomes a Cub he probably continues to do a certain amount of handicraft in school. This often gives to the Cubmaster who is not interested in this branch of our training, and who does not understand its uses, an excuse to neglect it entirely. " My Cubs don't like handicrafts. They get quite enough of that in school," is a cry that is frequently heard. This is quite true in a sense, but have they had any opportunity given them in school to develop their own imagination and their own initiative through handicrafts ? It is in that direction that the value of handicrafts as an aid to character training in the Pack lies ; and the Cubmaster who neglects this aid is making a great mistake. There is not the space to give specific illustrations, but I have known different boys in different Packs whose whole outlook on Cubbing, and on life in general for that matter, has been changed immensely for the better by their Akela's instigation to make something for themselves.

In the Pack we are more intent on teaching the boy to use his fingers, to develop his own imagination and natural ability, to occupy his spare moments at home, and to make little things for other people.

In the Troop we advance a stage further along the road, as should be the case with all our other activities. The boy is older and stronger, his tastes are forming, and so, while handicrafts help the Scout along these selfsame lines, in addition they help him to see the value and fun of hobbies, and may, possibly only as we have found, have an important bearing on his eventual vocation. Some dozen indoor handicrafts are dealt with in the Scout proficiency badges, but many other similar activities can be practised, indoors or out, which will interest and help.

To the Scoutmaster handicrafts are perhaps primarily useful as forming an adjunct to winter work and as providing an incentive to self-help, both in the case of the individual Scout and of the Troop. Some Troops specialise in a limited number of handicrafts, other Troops ring the changes very frequently. To a great extent the choice of the particular form of activity to be indulged in must be left to the Scouts themselves, so that their work is backed by their interest. The Court of Honour will soon be able to tell what this choice is. Sometimes the handicraft may be subsidiary to some other endeavour such as decorating Headquarters, or providing materials for a Scout Exhibition or Scout Fair. In these cases the choice is dictated by circumstances. In some cases handicrafts are utilised as a means of self-help, and Troops are able to support themselves on the sale of the various articles they have made. The selling can be done at a special exhibition, or a market can be obtained locally, or even at a distance, if the supply of articles is fairly constant. One Troop does a great deal by making fire-by-friction sets, another goes in for poker work of all kinds, another does leather work, another heraldic shields. There is no end to the different types of money-making handicrafts that can be adopted. Care must be taken, as has been done in all the Troops of which I am thinking at the moment, to see that these money-raising stunts are very much subordinated to the Scouting that the Troop is doing, and do not interfere with local trade.

In some cases, and these demand our particular attention, handicrafts are used not as a means of self-help, but as a means of helping others. Canada has given us a lead in this direction by the institution of toy-repair depots, where derelict toys are restored to their former new condition and distributed at Christmas time to the children of new settlers.

If definite handicrafts are adopted as a Troop activity, special classes, which can be conducted by outside helpers, will be necessary apart from normal Troop meetings. This is where the Troop with its own meeting-place scores so heavily, because the Troop Headquarters can be open every evening for those Scouts who want to come and do their bit. In country districts where the Scouts have to go long distances, it is possible to have special handwork before or after a meeting.

It might also be worth while mentioning the possibility of District, or even County Hobby Exhibitions. These have been a means of introducing many Scouters to handicrafts and the value of them in their Scout training, and also a means of showing the public what Scouts can do.

BOOKS.

*What Scouts Can Do*, Baden-Powell. Pearson, 2s. and 3s. 6d.
*Spare Time Activities*, " Gilcraft." Pearson, 1s. 6d. and 2s. 6d.
*Winter Crafts*, Cox and Gidney. Pearson, 1s. 6d. and 2s. 6d.

## CHAPTER XIII

### HOUSEKEEPING

WE may build a cheerful and comfortable house, we may furnish it well and wisely, we may decorate it inside and out, but unless we take some pains to set about the job of housekeeping in some kind of methodical way our house will be uncomfortable to live in, untidy in appearance, and will lose all interest and character.

It is the same with our Troop ; we can build it up from small beginnings ; we can gradually increase it in size and in standing ; we can collect a certain amount of gear for camp and various Scout practices ; but unless we introduce some method into our way of running things, and keep a careful eye on records and finance, our Troop may easily go to pieces. We are not in a position to hand it over to anyone else at any moment as a going concern.

Yet, like a house, our Troop should always be in order. We should know what it has, both as regards Scouts and gear. We should know where things are. We should have ordered in supplies ahead —this does not only refer to grub for camp but to ordinary gear, books, programmes and what not. Everything should run smoothly and well, and no mischance should be allowed to upset the order of things.

When we are staying in a well-run house, we do not see the machinery which brings the meals punctually to table, keeps everything tidy and so on, but we would soon notice the absence of it or realise when it was faulty. In a well-run Troop it is the same. The machinery is not apparent on the surface ; each one has his job and does it ; the Scoutmaster knows that everything is in order and up to date, he knows his larder is full—stocked not with food but with ideas, programmes, lists of games, future plans and all the other things which will continue to keep the Troop fit and in good fettle. Speaking generally, it is all a question of being prepared.

*Records*

There are a certain number of housekeeping books that the Scoutmaster has to maintain. There is a Troop Roll or Register to be kept up to date. This contains the names and certain information in regard to the members of the household—his Troop There are various printed forms available on which the information can be posted in regard to dates of admission, passing of tests and badges and other things of more or less routine nature. There is no reason why the Scoutmaster should keep this formal register himself ; an A.S.M. or a Scout can easily keep it posted up to date. There is scope for a useful Rover Scout job here.

The Scoutmaster should keep his own diary. If this is interleaved with the Troop Register, he will have to keep both himself, for very few of us like others to see our own private diary while we are still alive. This diary is alluded to in *Tracking Rules for Scouters*, a pamphlet that has already been mentioned. In his diary the Scoutmaster should keep his own private notes in regard to each boy in his Troop, making an attempt from time to time to sum up the character of each, to jot down the lines along which he intends to work with each, the response that they make to treatment. This is his case-book, and should contain the inner history of each Scout and his inner progress, as against his more outward progress in the matter of badges, but unless it is continually looked at and estimates revised it will be useless.

Other housekeeping books may be more briefly mentioned, not because they are unimportant, but because they are not quite of so much consequence as the Diary. There is no necessity for the Scoutmaster to keep any of the others himself, in fact from the point of view of training it is better that they should be maintained by the Scouts themselves.

E

Each Patrol Leader should have a Patrol Roll Book which he keeps up and submits from time to time to the Scoutmaster and the Court of Honour. The more he can be encouraged to add information to a bare list of attendances and subscriptions the better. He is in charge of certain members of the household and should set out to get to know all about them. Unless he jots this information down, he is liable to forget it or ignore it when it would be useful to his Scoutmaster.

A list of all that the Troop possesses in the way of gear, etc., should be kept. This is an inventory of the household's possessions and fixings. It is important that it should be maintained in case of changes of personnel, of fire, theft and of all the other accidents that may happen at any time to property. Not only should such a list be maintained, but there should be a clear understanding as to whom the property belongs. This is an essential precaution to take from the very beginning, whether in an open or in a controlled Troop. The Scoutmaster should himself see that some kind of a Deed of Trust is drawn up and that it is kept in safe custody. Imperial Headquarters will help when asked with a model Deed and with advice. This question of property is an important one and has been fruitful of trouble in the past. The inventory of property, or stock book, can be maintained by an Assistant, by a Rover Scout or by one of the Scouts themselves. Whoever maintains it, the Scoutmaster should see that a periodical official check is made by the Court of Honour. If we are training boys to become good citizens, it is part of our training that they should be taught business methods, and that they should learn that public property is to be respected. Once they begin to realise the value of the property the Troop possesses and what is involved in the way of responsibility by that possession, they will be better qualified to have their say in the collection and disposal of local and government funds and possessions later on.

As a further help in the business training of the Court of Honour there is the Court's Minute Book, which should be kept by one of the Patrol Leaders. Preferably the Court's Scribe should be changed every three months so that each of the Scout members has an opportunity of learning something about the keeping of minutes by actually doing the job. This is one of those little points which are liable to escape notice, more especially if we have a Scribe who is good at his job. We are apt to keep him at it because he is good, instead of displacing him by someone who is bad, but who will in all probability get better through practice.

Lastly there is a very important book—the Troop Log—important because it records the history and traditions of the Troop. Here again it should be a record of the Troop as seen from the Scout's point of view. All the entries in it should be made by Scouts, with an occasional contributed article by a Scouter on request. The Troop is the Scouts' ; its Log should be theirs too.

This will entail considerable encouragement and prompting on the Scoutmaster's part at first, but once it has been got going well there should not be so much difficulty in keeping it going. The Log should not be just a bare record of programmes and badges awarded. These should appear, but be written up in an interesting kind of way, special mention being made of anything very exciting and amusing. Chaff—especially of the Scouters—should be allowed and encouraged. It makes for a very happy family spirit if such chaff is taken in good part, and appreciated for what it is— a token of affectionate regard. Boys are not inclined to chaff those whom they do not like ; they are more apt to ignore them altogether. The Log should be illustrated too by any sketches or photographs that the Scouts like to contribute. If there is an artistic Scouter in the Troop, he may be invited to contribute a sketch now and then, especially if he can picture a landscape that the Troop likes, or can make a humorous drawing of some incident in camp. The Out-of-doors and Camp should bulk largely in every Troop's Log.

Such a book will not only be of value to the Troop itself, but will be of interest to parents, visiting Scouters and others. The activities and nature of the Troop should be reflected in it.

*Finance*

Money is one of the bugbears of housekeeping, and can easily become one of the Troop as well. The question of finance is dealt with in Rules 4 and 9 of *Policy, Organisation and Rules*, and these rules should be very carefully studied and followed by every Scoutmaster. Mention has already been made of the most scrupulous care that should be observed in respect of public property, and the same holds good in respect of public funds. All Troop funds, whether contributed entirely by the boys themselves or not, should be regarded and treated with the same care as public funds. In any case the Scoutmaster is well advised to have a separate Treasurer, and not to handle the Troop's finances himself. If money is subscribed by, or obtained from, the public, our Rules clearly lay down that it should be administered by the Group Committee. This is laid down as a safeguard both to the public and to the Scoutmaster, although some of the latter appear to regard it as an implication against their honour. None are so blind as those who will not see, and some are apt to ignore a helping hand as much as a fist until it lands, when they soon discover the difference. In such cases the Group Committee will have its own Treasurer, and there is no reason why he should not have custody of all the Group's funds, whether contributed by the boys or otherwise. There is a difference, however, in the disposal of these funds. The boys themselves should have the main say in the spending of the money that they have contributed in cash or in kind—by way of effort such as Displays and other entertainments for which they have been responsible. In these cases, unless there are serious reasons to the contrary, the Group Treasurer and Committee should accept any decision that the Court of Honour has made in regard to the disposal of the Scout's contributions. This does not prevent the Court voting money for some project in which the Committee are primarily interested, such as the building of a Troop Hut.

It is well worth the Scouter's while to explain something of the keeping of accounts to the Scouts themselves. No boy can learn too early in life the value of money, and the importance both of keeping a correct record of the money he receives and the money he spends, and of buying within his means so as not to run into debt.

The Group Committee should administer the funds for which they are responsible, but are under the obligation, unless the money has been raised for any specific purpose, of consulting the Scoutmaster, and through him the Court of Honour, as to the best outlay that can be made in order to further the Scouting of the Group.

The question of self-help, which has already been mentioned in the previous chapter, is an important one, since it concerns the character-building side of Scouting. It is quite obviously wrong for the adults connected with the Group to pay for everything. I know Troops which are equipped, so to speak, with all kinds of modern labour-saving devices ; I know Troops who have a bare minimum of equipment, and that mostly camp gear. I have no hesitation in saying that the latter type of Troop has always struck me as being the more Scoutlike in every particular. Such a Troop's tents may be old and patched, but they give a pride of possession which is to be envied.

Ways and means of raising the wind are many and various. One has already been mentioned, others will be alluded to in a subsequent chapter. There are undesirable ways which have been employed from time to time, and at the risk of treading on some people's toes I will mention one or two that occur to me now. Whist Drives and Dances are to be discouraged, unless the whole management of them is in the hands of the Group Committee, and the Scouts themselves have nothing to do with them, even so far as regards the selling of tickets. I do not, of course, include Rover Scouts in the term Scouts, that is a different matter. Raising money on Raffles, on articles such as Scent cards with an obviously inflated value savour to me of dishonesty. I will carefully steer round bazaars and such-like in case I get into hot water, but I would mention entertainments which do not give full value as undesirable means of raising funds for the Troop.

Proper accounts should be kept, and should be available for inspection by those who have contributed to the Group's finances. The Scouts themselves have the right to inspect the accounts where their own contributions are concerned, but normally it is sufficient the Court of Honour do this periodically as representing the Scouts.

It is advisable that within the Local Association some common form of account keeping should be adopted, as this will greatly facilitate any audit that the Local Association may care to make under Rule 9.

## Uniforms

One of the greatest problems of the householder is to keep the household clothed. In many Troops it is as urgent a problem to know by what means the Scouts should obtain their Scout uniforms. Normally each Scout should pay for his own uniform, but this is not always practicable. The financial standing of our Scouts differs very considerably, and we have to see to it that that does not make any outward difference to their Scouting, just as we know it makes no difference inwardly. These matters should be adjusted as between the Scout concerned and the Scoutmaster. It is not fair to the boy that the Court of Honour, which contains his pals, should discuss his family finances. In some Troops, especially those in poor neighbourhoods, certain articles of uniform are contributed from Group funds, usually hat, belt and scarf. These remain the property of the Group, and are handed back when the boy leaves the Group or obtains others. In other Troops a Clothing fund is maintained by the Scouters or by the Group Treasurer, the former being preferable so long as the running of it can be delegated to an A.S.M. The fund can be started by a permanent loan from the Group Committee, and is kept floating by the contributions that the Scouts pay in from time to time until their account is paid up : Uniform Account cards can be obtained from Imperial Headquarters. In other Troops grants in aid are made from Group funds to necessitous cases on the certificate of the Scoutmaster.

In one country Troop, whose Scoutmaster I know well, a boy, on passing his Tenderfoot tests, is rigged out by the Troop from its clothing store, but not with a completely new uniform. When he grows out of the various articles he returns them mended and clean, and gets larger sizes in exchange. No difficulty has been experienced in uniforms not being cared for, and the boys themselves know that the Troop as a whole has worked for the money that enables this to be done.

Another Troop maintains a Uniform fund out of which it purchases materials for various handicrafts—such as the wooden frames of stools. Materials are supplied free to a Scout, and on completion of the article by him the value of it is credited to his Uniform account irrespective of its date of sale. In this way the Scouts are enabled to work for their own uniforms.

All Badges should be paid for by the Local Association or the Scout Group and should remain their property, so that their return can be required if necessary.

*Group Committee*

The household usually has a small group of people who are consulted in difficulties—the Padre, Doctor, Solicitor, Banker. If a Scout Group has a similar group of people on whom it can depend for advice and help, it can obviously gather strength and continuity.

A Group Committee is obligatory when funds are obtained from outside sources, but it is a desirable adjunct to the Group or Troop in any circumstances. There has been trouble as between Scoutmaster and Committee in the past chiefly because no one has made any attempt to lay down what the functions of the Committee were. Their duties in regard to finance have already been mentioned ; it is also advisable that all Group property should be invested in them under a proper Deed of Trust. Apart from that they are concerned only in the outside business affairs of the Group and should not interfere with its internal workings. So far as the Troop is concerned the Scout work that it does is under the control of the Scoutmaster, subject only to the Group Scoutmaster if he is a separate individual. The Committee can only interfere when the Scout work of the Troop is obviously bad and contrary to rule and method. Even then they should not take the Troop into their own hands, but should bring the matter to the notice of the District Commissioner. There is never any trouble if, on the formation of a Committee, its functions are clearly laid down in writing and understood.

This does not mean that the Scoutmaster should ignore the Committee, however ; as a matter of courtesy, if nothing else, he should periodically let them know how the Troop is progressing, what its needs are, and what successes it, or individual members of it, have won. He should try and interest each member of the Committee in the Troop as a whole, and separate members in individual Scouts who can be helped in their future occupations thereby.

The composition of a Group Committee depends on circumstances, but the parents should be represented there, as well as influential and interested people of the neighbourhood. Mothers should not be ignored ; many Troops have found a Mothers' sub-committee a very useful ally.

There is one more function of the Group Committee that can be mentioned. It serves to widen the interest in Scouting and provides a number of people who can help in securing in the locality a real appreciation of what Scouting stands for generally, and who can help to popularise the Group in particular.

A Scoutmaster is greatly strengthened in all his doings if he has the knowledge that he has a loyal body of men and women ready to back him up to secure the real aims of Scouting.

## CHAPTER XIV

### THE DOMESTIC STAFF

To assist him in running the Troop the Scoutmaster has a staff of men and boys—Assistant Scoutmasters and Patrol Leaders. If this staff is to be of any assistance the members of it must be given various definite jobs to do and know what these jobs are. The Scoutmaster is like a housekeeper who looks after everyone in the house, sees that they are comfortable, sees that the various members of the staff have their allotted tasks and get on with them, sees that everyone works in together as one harmonious whole. In consequence the house is comfortable and well run, everything goes smoothly.

So it should be with the Troop.

First let us consider the Scoutmaster himself who is the head of the staff. There should be no hesitation on his part that he is head. Obviously if things are to go well and in one required direction there must be a leader who gives the final word. Apart from that the Scoutmaster has to remember that he alone is responsible for the Troop to the boys, to their parents and to Scouting at large. He cannot excuse himself on the plea that what is being done is the work of his Assistants or is a decision of the Court of Honour. It is his duty to see that nothing is done in connection with the Troop that is in any way contrary to, or different from, the main principles and methods of Scouting.

It is his duty then to decide what requires doing after consulting with the other members of the household, and consulting their interests. When the various duties have been decided upon, it is the Scoutmaster's duty to apportion them to the various members of his staff, and to see that they are done. He himself must take a part, and a leading part, in these duties.

In other words, if the Troop is to be conducted in a proper manner, it is necessary to pool the abilities and energies of all the helpers there are available, and then to introduce a certain amount of organisation into the running of the Troop.

The various duties and responsibilities that the Scoutmaster should himself assume are mentioned throughout the whole of this book. They cannot possibly be compressed into a few short paragraphs. The qualifications required of him are set out in Rule 45, and all Commissioners and Local Associations are asked to be particularly careful to see that these qualifications are possessed by all persons applying for a Scoutmaster's warrant.

### *Assistant Scoutmasters*

Rule 11 has already been quoted to show that an Assistant Scoutmaster is required for every Troop, and more than one if the Troop consists of more than three Patrols. The qualifications A.S.M.'s should possess are the same as for a Scoutmaster with the exception of ability to secure the use of some sort of clubroom. They may, however, receive a warrant at the age of eighteen as opposed to the Scoutmaster's twenty.

When looking round for Assistants the S.M. would do well to start by laying down to himself a higher age than that mentioned, so that he may be able to secure the help of a man who has already had some experience of the world. This question of age is rather an important one. I hope it will be understood that I am far from decrying the average young man, but it should be obvious that if we are aiming to train up a boy to be a good citizen it is rather important that we should have some practical experience of citizenship to go upon. Theories are all very well, but they do not stand the stress of time or of difficulty. If we are going to advise boys as to the future livelihood they should adopt, we should have some considerable experience of the ways and means of earning a living ourselves. Sometimes a Scouter is rather like the " Aunt Julia " of a popular paper who blissfully advises young girls about their love affairs and intimate details of their lives, while pulling hard at his pipe in an upstairs office in Fleet Street, his knowledge of young girls being confined to seeing them get in and out of trains and buses. ·

That is somewhat of a digression I am afraid, so let us get on with the choice of an A.S.M. The Scoutmaster would be well advised not to look for someone who has similar tastes and abilities as he himself possesses. His Assistant need not necessarily help simply by copying all his tastes and methods ; he can be of more help if he brings other gifts to the common treasury, so that the two between them can make a really good Scoutmaster. It is impossible to say more in regard to choice in any general kind of way, but we can be quite definite in regard to the relationship that should exist between a Scoutmaster and his A.S.M.'s. Obviously that relationship should be one of mutual respect which will lead to real friendship. They have the common bond of the Troop and a liking for boys, and should be co-partners in everything that is done, the senior partner, as has been said, making the final decision whenever one is necessary.

The duties that can be delegated to an A.S.M. depend naturally on the personalities and abilities of the Scouters concerned. At first it will be necessary to discuss what each is best qualified to do and to apportion work and responsibilities accordingly. It is important that some definite delegation be made by the Scoutmaster so that his hands are not always full of petty details. On the other hand it is not fair that the A.S.M. should be given just the petty and dirty jobs to do, while the S.M. gets all the jam, so to speak. All future work and plans should be discussed together, and the A.S.M.'s advice should be sought and adopted whenever it appears to indicate the better course to take.

A certain amount of the business side of the Troop in regard to records and finance can be taken over by an A.S.M., but it is not only on the material side of Scouting that he can help. His co-operation should be invited on the character-training side as well. Character judging and character training is one of the most difficult jobs there are, and the Scoutmaster needs all the help he can get. The Troop as a whole and individual members of it should be continually discussed over a friendly fire, or in the quiet of a night in camp. These are the times when Scouters can get together, and get to grips with their real job. If a Troop of four Patrols has two A.S.M.'s it is a good plan to ask each to pay particular attention to two Patrols, as well as keeping a general eye on the Troop as a whole.

If a Scoutmaster has no Assistants, he has obviously a more difficult job to tackle. He may be able to secure the services of a Rover Scout or of someone else who has not the aptitude or time to undertake the obligations of a warrant. With this help he is in a stronger position, but all the time he should be on the look-out for an A.S.M., and should realise, too, that it is quite possible that one may be found from amongst the Scouts of his own Troop. Many a good Scouter has been lost because a Scouter did not look near enough home. Some of us find it so difficult to realise that boys grow up and become men.

### Troop Leader

Special provision is made in Rule 32 for the appointment of a Troop Leader, who must have been a Patrol Leader for not less than six months, and must also be a First-class Scout. It is not necessary that the office should be filled in every Troop, nor is it necessary that the Troop Leader should be without a Patrol of his own. If one Patrol Leader obviously stands out above the others, it is only fitting that his merit should be recognised. If it is desired to give responsibility to more boys, then one of the P.L.'s can become Troop Leader and his Patrol be taken over by another.

The right Troop Leader is one of the most important members of the Domestic Staff. He can back up all the Scoutmaster's efforts and set the tone for all the Scouts to adopt. Like the head boy in a school he is frequently able to get down to the roots of things better than the Scouters, and his advice is, therefore, invaluable. He can act as the Leader of the Patrol Leaders and help them over their difficulties. A good Troop Leader will make a good Assistant Scoutmaster before very long. The position should not, therefore, be used as a kind of shelf on which to place an older, and not very useful, Patrol Leader. It demands the best Scout there is in the Troop. It is not fair to dismiss the Troop Leader as a kind of Storekeeper or odd-job man. He can do much more than that in training Patrol Leaders, running the inter-Patrol Competition, and influencing the Troop as a whole.

*Patrol Leaders*

A good deal has already been said in one way or another in regard to Patrol Leaders, including various methods of selection and appointment. They are important members of the Scoutmaster's staff, and are, in fact, the backbone of the Troop. The Troop is run as a joint affair for the benefit of the Scouts, and not for the benefit of the Scouters, and the Patrol Leaders as representing the Scouts should have a real say in its government. The Patrol is a complete unit in itself led by the Patrol Leader, who owes allegiance to the Scoutmaster and the Court of Honour. It is essential that every opportunity of exercising leadership should be afforded, and that various duties in connection with the Troop as a whole should be delegated to them, such as Scribe, Storeman, Camp-fire Leader.

The Patrol Leaders should be led to see that they have an important part in the welfare of the Troop, that their advice is welcome at all times, that their view can frequently be adopted. The Scoutmaster has to remember, even when he denies it, that these boys are likely to know more about the other boys of the Troop than he does. They probably consort with them at school or at work, they know their brothers and sisters, and so on. Being boys themselves they can tell him a great deal about their point of view. A Scoutmaster who never listens to his Patrol Leaders, or who disregards them, will never make a success of his job. A Scoutmaster who says that he cannot get his Patrol Leaders to utter a word is engaged on the wrong kind of social work ; his *métier* lies elsewhere ; he has not the requisite point of contact with boys ; that is all, but it is everything so far as a Scouter is concerned.

A certain amount of independence on the part of Patrol Leaders is to be encouraged. They should gather their Patrols together at other times than at Troop meetings. If they maintain a certain amount of mystery in regard to these Patrol gatherings, well and good ; they have probably some surprise to spring later on. Patrol expeditions, Patrol camps are all to be encouraged as making for keener Patrols and better Scouting. The Scoutmaster can supervise a certain amount, but he should not be continually spying round to see what his Patrols and his Patrol Leaders are about. His job is to try and fire his Leaders with the fact of their responsibility for the Scouting abilities of each member of their Patrols and to let them see that he is reposing trust and confidence in them. This need not be expected all at once, but it can undoubtedly be attained to in every normal Scout Troop.

As a help to his Leaders the S.M. should run an instructional Patrol of which he is P.L. and his A.S.M.'s, T.L. and P.L.'s members. It is best if this Patrol has a name and totem, and so can secure something of an atmosphere and tradition. This is not only a training Patrol where the P.L.'s are practised in the games and exercises that are going to take place in the Troop, but is also an experimental Patrol where various ideas are tried out. This Patrol becomes in fact the Troop's laboratory and can be extremely useful accordingly. It is probably best that the Patrol meets once a fortnight, the alternate weeks being occupied by meetings of the Court of Honour. If possible, the meetings of the Patrol and of the Court should be held on a different night of the week to that devoted to Troop meetings ; otherwise the meetings should take place after the Troop meeting has dispersed, and the Scouts have gone home.

## The Court of Honour

The staff council is the Court of Honour which manages the internal business affairs of the Troop as well as protecting its traditions and its standards. Normally the Scoutmaster is the Chairman of the Court, though in many Troops it has been found possible to allow one of the P.L.'s to take the chair. Personally I prefer the Scoutmaster in the chair, because the ultimate responsibility for the well-being of the Troop rests with him. The other Scouters of the Troop and the P.L.'s are members, one of the latter in turn acting as Scribe. In large Troops which have a number of A.S.M.'s it is sometimes advisable that they should not all be members of the Court, as their presence is likely to overbalance the representation of boys. It is a good plan to keep a minimum balance of two boys to each grown-up. In small Troops with only a couple of Patrols, Seconds may also be members of the Court.

The procedure to be followed at these meetings, which should be conducted in a business-like yet Scouty way, is somewhat as follows. I give the actual procedure adopted by a certain Troop :

> Minutes of Last Meeting—signed by assent.
> Business arising out of Minutes.
> Each Patrol Leader makes report on Patrol.
> Past and Future Programmes discussed.
> Duties for fortnight arranged.
> General Business and Suggestions.
> Prayers.

This procedure shows the functions of the Court in its administrative capacity and is self-explanatory.

When the traditions and standards of the Troop are concerned, the functions of the Court of Honour take on a different tone. For instance, here is the procedure observed by the same Troop when a candidate is recommended by a Scouter or P.L. for admission to the Troop :

The boy must be supported by a member of the Troop who has at least one year's service.

Candidate introduced by his supporter.

Candidate's answers to questions by any member of Court noted.

Candidate retires.
Candidate's answers discussed.      ·
Voting by secret ballot, S.M. acting as scrutinizer.
Candidate recalled and informed of result.
Each member of Court signs name in Court's Minute-book.

When, however, any Scout is brought before the Court because of unscoutlike behaviour, it should be an understood principle that his Patrol Leader and the Scoutmaster have both spoken to him, independently and together. Appearance before the Court should be the last resort so far as discipline is concerned. Petty difficulties and differences should not be brought before it. On such occasions the Court should not ape a judicial court too much. It is a Court of Enquiry based on a sincere desire to help the Scout at fault, not to punish him. The Troop as a whole is concerned, because when that Scout was invested, the Troop collectively accepted responsibility for him, and promised to help him throughout his Scout journey. There are occasions when hearts have to be hardened and a boy removed for the good of the others, but the Scoutmaster and the members of the Court have to realise first that that particular boy needs Scouting more than the others as a general rule, and that removal is absolutely the last resort. The whole subject is rather a complicated one and impossible to solve in a few sentences.

If some such methods and attitudes as are explained in this chapter are adopted by the Scoutmaster he will find that his Troop is unified, that his own work is made easier, that he has more time to devote to the study of the Scouts themselves, that the keenness of the Patrols merges into the good of the Troop, and that a happy family feeling is engendered which finds expression in the term, OUR TROOP.

BOOKS.

*Problems of a Patrol Leader*, Braham. Pearson, 6d.
*How to run a Patrol*, Lewis. Brown, 9d.

# CHAPTER XV

### THE FAMILY

THE Scoutmaster has to look after and care for all the Scouts in his Troop, collectively and individually. It is a large family he has on his hands, but he should regard them all as his Scout family. They are noisy and troublesome at times, but they are full of enthusiasm, of love of the heroic and adventurous, of generous trust, and respond quickly to the calls that are made on them. So they bring a reward for hard work and prolonged thought, provided, as always, that the proper atmosphere is in evidence.

The Scoutmaster wrestles with the problems of his family, with the characters of the individual boys in the family ; he thinks, prays, longs, plans in regard to each one of them in the same way as a father or mother might do. Unless the Scoutmaster is able to assume that kind of a relationship to his boys, the Scouting that he does with them is liable to be something that affects outward appearances only, and that does not penetrate down into the depths of their beings as is intended. Numbers, efficiency and so on are as nothing unless the real spirit of Scouting is also there.

First of all there is the question of control to be considered. The Scoutmaster has to exercise control over his Troop and the members of it, and a great deal depends on the method he adopts. Some can do this entirely in the right way by instinct, but most of us have to learn by degrees and by repeated trials and failures. Some exercise control by using their personality only, which is all very well so far as they themselves are concerned, but is rather bad luck on their helpers and successors. If we depend for our control on personality alone, it is likely to become a somewhat transient quality.

If we are to make a real success of our endeavours to control boys and to further their development, we must give the subject some consideration and endeavour to acquire certain qualities which will help us.

The successful Scouter, then, must have the ability to place himself on the right plane with his boys as a first step, and must possess something of the Boy Spirit himself. He must acquire —chiefly by experience—some knowledge of the varying characteristics of boys at different ages. He must make use of discovery methods in trying out each boy and discovering what is in him with a view to eliminating the bad by encouraging the good. He must promote a corporate spirit among all the Scouts in the Troop in order to gain the best results. This last is merely a reiteration of what has already been said in regard to the Patrol system and the other Scouters of the Troop.

So far as the right plane is concerned, it may be taken for granted that the Scout expects a Scouter to be genuine and modest and to have superior ability and power. On the Scouter's part this must all be real, for the Scout will readily see through a mere veneer of modesty and ability. If possible, and so far as the average Scouter is concerned it is not impossible, he should be able to do some one thing or other really well. Whatever his mental or physical abilities may be, the Scouter who can live the life of his boys in camp and otherwise will find very little difficulty in making a success of the average Troop. The Scouter who pretends, or who is afraid of his Troop, will find great difficulty in achieving any kind of success.

No two boys are alike, and so no one set of rules or general principles can be blindly applied to the handling of boys. It is quite beyond the majority of us to guess what move the boy's

interests or thoughts will prompt him to take. We can make a
guess perhaps, and in course of time, as we gain experience, our
guesses may approximate to what actually will happen, and that
depends on a variety of factors usually hidden from our view.
For instance, the same talk may bore one boy to death, and fire
another with enthusiasm ; it may bore the boy to death in one
mood, and inspire the same boy in another mood. So it is that
we must proceed warily and carefully along our trail, observing,
comprehending and analysing all the signs that appear upon it.

One important fact that we have to realise is that most of the
important decisions in a boy's life are made between the ages of
fourteen and eighteen. His character is being built up, but character is an animate thing which is contagious ; it is caught more
than taught—in the same way as religion. If a group of boys is
exposed to a man of strong character they will tend to become
like him, even if they have been exposed to his influence only for
a short time. It is what we do and are that counts more than what
we say. Mention has already been made of individuality as one
of the important materials to be used in our building of the Scout
home ; it is just as essential a material in the development of the
Scout family.

We have to realise that a boy, though capable of reasoning, *acts*
not on reason but on impulse. The boy can give excellent reasons
in the abstract for what his conduct should be, but when it comes
to action this conduct will be largely governed by impulse. As
the boy develops reason will gradually take a larger place in his
actions ; but not till he is fully grown up will it dominate. This
emphasises the importance of cultivating good influences, and of
giving good directions to vague energies.

If you tell a boy how important self-control is, he will very
likely agree with you, but let a little excitement come in and there
will not be much sign of the desired quality. There is some chance,
however, of increasing his self-control if he is encouraged to play
such games as Creep Mouse, Freezing, Blind Pirate or Stalking,
because he cannot make a success of any such games without
unconsciously using self-control.

Another matter of importance is that we should realise that boys
do not develop regularly and equally. A boy may suddenly lose
all interest in what he has enjoyed for some time past. This is
not fickleness, but the natural way in which his mind develops.
It is not a question of his mind going up an inclined plane, but
up a pyramid with steep, uneven steps. Sometimes one of these
steps leads to a period of unruliness, and the boy becomes defiant,
difficult and rude. These symptoms must be discouraged, but at
the same time great patience must be exercised. For no apparent
reason there may be another sudden change, and the aggressive,
difficult boy becomes helpful and orderly. Very likely he is quite
unconscious that he was anything else during the difficult period.

Some boys become apparently sullen, others slightly hysterical, others clumsy and shy. The danger is that we get annoyed with them because they are not the " nice little boys " of eleven ! Unspoken sympathy will do much to help, coupled with plenty of activity and responsibility.

Then again it will be found that every natural boy demands advancement. He longs to be a little older than he is, he longs to know a little more than he does, he longs to be able to do more than he can. We can use this desire, but must not speed it up. Gradual development is what the boy needs for his future welfare, not any kind of forced, unnatural growth. The programme of activities that we offer the boy must recognise the principle of progression, and so will appeal to the boy. The programme that we offer must also contain something for the older boy that is different from what is offered to the younger boy. This sounds difficult until it is realised that responsibility as Patrol Leader, as Second and so on, goes a long way to meet the older boy's needs.

Then the Scouter has to remember that the law of interest is deep in the roots of boy nature. His problem is to create and maintain interest, sometimes to replace desires by better ones made to appear so attractive as unconsciously to displace undesirable ones. There are various ways in which the problem can be solved, and there are certain words that give the key to various solutions —action, out-of-doors, surprise, mystery, the unusual, the doing of things, initiative. At one time or another something has been said in this book on each one of these points, but I would say more on the question of initiative.

The exercise of initiative by the Scouts themselves, though taking more time, though more difficult to control and supervise, is more full of results than any formal subordination of the Scouts to the Scouter with all its seeming quickness and convenience. The Scouter must realise that the older the boy becomes, the more and more must adult influence become advisory—giving way to the captaincy of the boy over himself.

Having ranged somewhat widely and discursively over the field of boy nature, it is time to set down one or two lines of general treatment that the Scouter can adopt.

Obviously kindness and sympathy are better than sternness, but we have to realise, as already mentioned in discussing the subject of discipline, that weakness is no sign of either kindness or sympathy. Any suspicion of favouritism and any tendency towards sloppishness or mawkish sentimentality must be rigorously avoided. Genuine interest in, enjoyment of, and time for, the things which the boy himself enjoys are the keynotes to success. The Scouter has to think with the mind of the Scout, to put himself in his place. This is the only way in which to track him down, to discover his aims and desires. It is quite natural for a young boy, whose mind is maturing, to do remarkable, and at times unreasonable things. When such things as that happen there is no need for us to get worried or alarmed. On the contrary it is fairly safe to say that the boy who never does anything wrong or mischievous is either sick, or his will has been broken. Whatever the cause may be it needs our sympathy and treatment.

So what the Scouter has to do is to be fair, just and considerate so far as each boy in his Troop is concerned. He has to try and understand him, to study his habits and characteristics. The boy who is discouraged must be heartened ; the boy who is slow or weak must be encouraged ; the boy who is quick-tempered must be restrained ; the boy who is a boaster must be taken down a peg in a friendly but firm fashion ; the boy who gives himself airs must be brought down to earth, sometimes even with a bump ; the boy who is mischievous must be kept busy and occupied ; the boy who has marked ability must be given responsibility so that he can advance farther ; that boy who has no marked ability must be given opportunities to prove to himself that he can do things, and some small responsibility to prove to him that he is trusted ; the boy who is forgetful must receive special training in details such as Kim's Games ; the boy who is inclined to be silly must be associated with the more sensible Scouts who are in a position to be able to cure him.

It is to be remembered that the boy's present habits are not necessarily lasting ones. Habits are built up, new replace old almost unconsciously if the new are made more attractive, while old habits die quickly if they cause discomfort. Sometimes a boy is in grip of a bad habit, which he cannot break unless his will is reinforced by someone else's will. With real sympathy it is possible for the Scouter to induce the boy to go into partnership with the best that is in himself and make a fight for it, knowing that the Scouter is there to back him up in his struggle and to sympathise with him even in his failures.

Volumes have been written on this subject of boy nature ; it is quite impossible to deal with it in the scope of a few pages. My object has been more to get Scouters thinking along certain lines, to convey an attitude, rather than to attempt the impossible and tell them how to control and develop the boys of their Troops.

## CHAPTER XVI

### THE FAMILY GROWS UP

THE Scouter is frequently faced with the problem of how to help one of his Scouts to come to a decision in taking up some particular activity in Scouting, whether it be some kind of outdoor work, a Proficiency Badge, or a form of Handicraft. Here is one of those golden opportunities which Scouting provides for the Scouter who has the welfare of his boys at heart, and who has the good sense to give each one of his boys patient and careful individual study. By personal contact, judicious questioning and observation he can generally arrive at an understanding of each boy's likes and dislikes, abilities and deficiencies. By the continual tracking of these down, and marking of them up, he can discover whether the boy shows signs of being proficient in any particular line, he can bring out inherent traits and can arrange for the cultivation of any which may prove of use.

The young boy is very susceptible to judicious criticism ; but discriminating praise is frequently better than even constructive criticism. We have to use our own judgment coupled with our knowledge of the particular boy's characteristics. Slavish praise will often result in a swelled head and loss of ambition. We should be able to deal with him in such a manner that the boy will respond with the best that is in him, encouraging every effort with a quiet spoken word of praise, and indicating a possibly fresh line of attack.

The age when particular attributes become apparent varies considerably. We have to beware of calling a boy " stupid " or " dull " if he does not show some early signs of ability to do something particularly well. Each boy has to be treated on his own merits, and to be dealt with as a separate problem. He should not necessarily be compared with any other and held up to disparagement accordingly.

There is good in every boy if we can but find it.

Patrol Leaders can be of great assistance to their Scouters in such matters. They are in much closer personal touch with the boys of their Patrols. Frequently a modest boy will display some particular talent or ability to his Patrol mates, when he would not dream of doing so to his Scouter, or in presence of the Troop. So Patrol Leaders should be encouraged to know their Scouts and confide in their Scoutmaster, and Scoutmasters should consult their Patrol Leaders on all questions connected with the boys.

### Employment of Scouts

Most boys are with us in Scouting before they leave school, and a Scouter who does not consider how he can best help each one of his Scouts in regard to his life's work is largely failing in his duty to the Troop.

The tragedy in so many instances is that nothing is done in the matter until a boy leaves school, and the first step taken is when the boy comes along one day and says : " Please, Sir, Mother says can you help me get a job," whereas this should have been under consideration for at least twelve months before.

Thanks to the variety of interests in Scouting, by the time a boy has been in the Troop twelve months his Scouter should have a good idea of the type of career he is best suited for, either mechanical, commercial, professional, scientific or artistic. If he can help him to obtain employment where his best abilities and

F

enthusiasms will be united with his daily work, he will have done much to lay the foundations of the boy's future success and happiness, and also be helping him in a large extent to allay much of the unrest and discontent existing in industry to-day. If the boy's occupation is merely a means of earning a living, and the work he loves is side-tracked into his leisure hours or pushed out of his life altogether, he will only be the fraction of the man he ought to be.

One of the main dangers to be avoided is that the boy should not leave school without any prospect of work, and be left to his own devices to fill in his time away from the discipline of school and often with very little parental control. Under these conditions he is in real danger of getting into undesirable company, either of other unemployed or, what is worse, of the unemployable. If he can start on any kind of employment, he at least learns the self-discipline of having to keep time on his job and of some service being expected of him each day. These help in building up his character, instead of it degenerating by the fact of his being unwanted and of having no objective in his daily life.

One of the primary factors in enabling a Scouter to be of service in helping a boy to find his vocation in life is to know his parents and his home conditions and his schoolmaster, as every real Scouter should do, not only because it helps so much in obtaining the co-operation of his parents and his teacher, but also because it helps in gauging the boy's possibilities and the prospects open to him.

It should be quite clear that parents are primarily responsible for the employment undertaken by their boys, just as they are primarily responsible for seeing that the boy obtains the right knowledge that will guard him against evil at the critical periods of his life.

So in all cases consultation with parents is advisable before making any definite suggestions to a Scout. The Scoutmaster should keep a list of the dates when Scouts are likely to be leaving school, and should try and talk the matter over with his parents and schoolmaster at least a term before the boy is due to leave. He can also give occasional talks on the subject of employment at Parents' Socials, or even send round a short list of possible local openings, together with a brief summary of Scout Migration Schemes, particulars of which can be obtained by any Scout or Scouter from Imperial Headquarters. If advisable, such a list might also mention any organisations offering special facilities to Scouts, such as Naval and Mercantile Marine Training Schools, the Royal Air Force and the Royal Engineers.

The Scouter's special attention should be directed towards preventing Scouts taking up what are known as " blind alley " jobs. These are jobs where there is no possible chance of advancement, and which lead to unemployment after three or four years. It would not be fitting to indicate definite jobs of such nature here, but it is quite easy to discover them if a few judicious enquiries into the future are made.

When a boy leaves the Elementary School, and, as is often the case, has to take the first job available for economic reasons, even if it is a " blind alley " occupation, there is not so much harm as is usually imagined, provided someone interested in his welfare is on the look-out for his development in certain interests and can help him in due course to obtain employment in the direction of those interests. The boy himself should also be continually encouraged to keep on preparing himself for the future so that he can snatch at any opportunity for advancement that offers. On the other hand, having obtained a job, there is a natural tendency to let things slide for a bit until it is too late.

Again, it is most important that boys should be encouraged to continue their studies after leaving school by attending, where possible, the various evening classes that are held during the winter. They may feel that the particular job on which they are engaged is more or less that of a labourer, say, and that they need not worry about learning things which do not seem to affect their work ; but the extra knowledge gained by attending classes will most certainly prove useful to them in the long run, and they should if possible choose for study the subjects in which they are most interested.

The Scoutmaster, however, should do what he can to see that the boy is attending classes which—even indirectly—will fit him for his career, and is not just wasting time which is, it is a regrettable fact, a somewhat common occurrence.

The fact that a boy has attended, or is attending, evening classes is likely to impress a prospective employer favourably.

Attendance at Troop meetings will of course suffer, and it will often be Patrol Leaders and Seconds who are affected. However keen the Scouter is on having a full attendance at Troop nights, he must consider the boys' future, and should in all cases advise them to go to the classes, counting attendance there as attendance at the Troop, even though this course may prove to be to the detriment of the Troop. It may be possible to hold the Troop meeting on, say, Monday one week and Wednesday the next, so that those who attend classes on Monday will not be away from all Troop meetings throughout the winter.

Another factor which should also be made use of, and one with which the Scouter should always seek to co-operate, is the Juvenile Employment Bureau, for—although a Government department— their officials are very human and welcome a co-operation which can be mutually helpful. Mention has also been made of the schoolmasters with whom contact should always be made in regard to the boys' welfare.

Considerable help can also be rendered by the Scout Group Committee, or by individual members of it, and in the towns by the Local Association.

In some Local Associations it is found possible to run a Scout Employment Bureau, but if this is done it should always be in co-operation with the Government one and with the general body of Scouters. Our aim is to be allies of education and employment departments, and not in any sense competitors. If the town also possesses a Rotary Club it will usually be found that its members are only too willing to help with advice as to the qualifications required for their various businesses and to notify vacancies to the Bureau or to individual Scouters.

A useful asset in connection with vocational guidance for Scouts is to arrange from time to time for business men (again Rotarians will often help in this) to visit a Troop or an Association gathering of older Scouts and talk to them about their own business or profession. Another method is to arrange for individual interviews for boys who feel they are attracted to some particular business. This enables the boy to learn more of what will be required of him, and either stimulates his interest or possibly puts him off when he learns that the work is somewhat different to what he expected. In this way a boy may be prevented from taking up a line which would become a drudgery to him in after years.

All this points to the necessity of the Scouter establishing contact with local employers. Opportunities differ according to local circumstances, but in all cases the co-operation of Scouters is much appreciated by employers, and may result not only in sympathetic consideration of Scout enquiries, but also in increased local interest in the Scout Movement and in offers of instruction and advice on different subjects.

Any recommendation that a Scouter makes to an employer should be honest, such as the employer can rely on. The recommendation could with advantage be supported by a copy of the boy's Scout history. The Scouter can also, as has already been suggested, interview the employer, ascertain the type of boy required and the duties required of him, the prospects of the opening, and so on, so as to assure himself that the job is the right one for the Scout and the Scout is the right boy for the job.

One of the great things to be borne in mind when interviewing employers is to be careful not to overrate a Scout's abilities or cover up his faults—which we all possess, but to give a straightforward and genuine account of the boy. It will be found then that employers will come back to consult the Scoutmaster when they require further boys, having learnt that a Scout recommendation is a genuine one. The Scouter will also be able to go and see them again about any particular boy in the certain knowledge that any difficulty or hardship he may disclose will be given every consideration.

Finally we have to consider our relations with the boy himself and our responsibility towards him when he is just about to start employment.

It is one of the great moments in the boy's life ; and a quiet yarn with his Scoutmaster the night before he starts work may make all the difference to his career. A boy may be inspired by a right attitude towards work, be warned of the dangers of the workshop, etc., and encouraged to carry out the Scout Law despite the fresh difficulties he will encounter. One such boy gained strength by tacking a copy of the Scout Law inside the lid of his tool chest in the works, a fact which his Scoutmaster knew nothing about until the boy's employer told him of it and of how he appreciated that boy's character.

This is one of these moments which a Scoutmaster should never miss.

The menace of unemployment, with its attendant evils of slackness and lack of desire for work, is one against which all Scouters should do their utmost to safeguard their Scouts. It is only by thinking and planning ahead that they will be able to do so. It should not be a lone task; they should enlist the help and cooperation of as many as possible—parents, schoolmaster, doctor, padre, committee, the boy himself.

## CHAPTER XVII

### ANNUAL REPAIRS

MENTION was made in Chapter IV of the necessity for having some kind of a meeting-place for the Troop and the desirability of Scouts having a place of their own was alluded to. It is obviously impossible to lay down any standards to which Troop Headquarters should conform. They range in size and quality from large halls with subsidiary rooms, through old army huts and temporary buildings to attics and cellars. Some are the possession of the Troop and vested in the Group Committee, some are the property of the controlling authority, some are loaned or hired from church or school, some are let at a nominal rent by a sympathiser, some have been built by the Scouts themselves, some have been erected with funds raised by the Scouts themselves, some have been erected with loans which still require to be paid off. All these differing conditions impose different obligations and permit of differing uses.

The ideal Troop Headquarters is a room of sufficient size for the Troop to play indoor games, properly ventilated and heated so that bad air does not lead to inattention and restlessness, and cold air to chills, which the Scouts have worked for themselves in some way or other, which is open to them on most nights of the week, and which they are allowed to decorate as the Court of Honour decides. I propose to take this kind of an ideal Headquarters and suggest how it should be equipped and decorated in the hopes that Scouters who do not possess the ideal may see some way of utilising these suggestions in the Headquarters their Troops use.

The title of the chapter is somewhat misleading, but all the same we should try and achieve some change in the appearance, decoration or equipment of the Troop Headquarters every year. It may not be necessary to renew the whole scheme each year, but some change or other keeps interest alive, gives an opportunity for the Scouts to discuss the whole question, gives a certain amount of variety and employment. Every three years or so, in order to give education to the existing Scouts of the Troop, it is a good plan to redecorate the whole room.

Many of us can remember the fun we all had in fitting out some kind of a place in which to do our Scouting ; it is a pity that the Scouts who come after us should be denied that kind of fun in their turn. It is a sound idea, then, periodically to discuss and decide on some definite scheme of arrangement and decoration.

The first requirement is to set apart corners or sections of the room which Patrols can definitely call their own. Some Troops are lucky enough to have a number of small rooms available for this purpose. Other Troops are able to allot a corner of the room to each Patrol, each Patrol being allowed to take charge of the walls up to a length of some 5 feet from the corner. Sometimes it is possible to use folding screens so as to give Patrol corners a certain amount of seclusion. Two-fold screens, each half being 5 feet by 5 feet, are quite suitable for this purpose. These screens should be so hinged that they can be folded up flat against the walls when more space is required. On the outside they should be decorated a uniform colour to fit in with the room as a whole with the addition of the Patrol emblem. In place of screens swinging rods carrying curtains, made even of sacking—which can be painted and decorated—are quite useful. In a long narrow room I have seen one side divided into four compartments by the use of roller blinds, an idea which proved very workmanlike and effective. However the division is made it should be left to the Patrol concerned to decorate the inside of its particular compartment as it desires, subject to any veto or censorship that the Scoutmaster may impose. If the Patrol specialises in any particular subject that subject might be illustrated by diagrams, descriptions, pictures, examples. This kind of a scheme is illustrated in the Troop Room at Gilwell Park. Some kind of a record board for the Patrol, a picture of the Patrol animal or bird, pictures of the Patrol in past days, photographs of camp may also adorn the walls.

The scheme adopted for the room as a whole will be according to taste, but anything very elaborate should be avoided as well as framed pictures which are liable to get broken. If something of the atmosphere of the out-of-doors can be introduced so much the better. So far as possible the decorating should be done by the Scouts themselves, although any specially talented Scout or Scouter may be allowed more scope. Yellows and greens will be found to lend themselves to decoration better than other colours, but brightness and cheerfulness should prevail, and so any over-elaboration should be avoided. If the room or building has a character of its own, some attempt should be made to incorporate that character in the scheme of decoration chosen.

On the walls of every Troop room should be found a copy of the Scout Law, a chart showing the Scout progress of each member of the Troop, a place where notices can be pinned, and, if possible, pictures of the King and of the Chief Scout. Apart from the pictures, these adornments should be of home manufacture. The Scout Law can be painted or lettered out on a strip of linen or parchment, or painted on the wall itself, if the room is in the sole possession of the Group. If others use the room during the day or on other nights, it is still frequently possible for the two pictures and the Scout Law to be permanent features. A notice board can easily be made out of three-ply or stout cardboard painted green and framed with twigs. A green baize notice board seems out of place in a Scout room. The progress chart is easily drawn out and can be mounted on rollers so that it can be taken down when required.

If the Troop is forbidden to leave up any of its own decorations, but a few nails in convenient places are arranged for, it is possible for Patrols to bring and remove their particular decorations, and for the duty Patrol to look after the general decorations or charts.

Amongst other items that may be regarded as necessities are a Union Jack and a Troop flag or standard. The Union Jack should be broken and saluted at the beginning of every Scout meeting and lowered at the end. A flagstaff is not necessary, although it adds to effect, especially if it is rough-hewn, since an inconspicuous pulley or eye-screw in the roof and a set of halyards will fly the flag quite as effectively. Some Troops even have to reeve and unreeve the halyards every meeting, but there is an important psychological effect in overcoming such difficulties as these that has its own peculiar value in the training of the Scouts. The Troop standard should have a special place allotted to it, and can again be kept in the custody of the duty Patrol Leader or some near-by Scout during the week.

A blackboard is not necessary, since backs of old placards and advertisements, or brown paper and white chalk, will serve the purpose equally well.

The question of seats is of some importance. If the Troop merely occupies the room on sufferance, so to speak, one or two evenings in the week, it has to put up with what there is. If, however, it has more permanency of possession, then it can instal

its own furniture. This should not be elaborate. A table and
chair, at which the Scouters, Troop Scribe, and others can sit
down and write up records and returns, are more than useful.
Apart from that it is advisable to avoid ordinary chairs and benches
which are apt to take up a great deal of room and to get broken
in a rowdy game. Some Troops have managed to acquire log
seats for each member of the Troop; these are normally kept in
Patrol corners and moved about when required. Other Troops
have made use of margarine boxes, painted in green or in Patrol
colours, with a hole in the top through which a finger can be
inserted for carrying. Patrol Leaders and Scouters are allowed
special colours, or even sizes. Some Troops have combined boxes
for gear with seats, each Patrol having a box in its corner for
Patrol gear which also serves as the P.L.'s seat. Rope handles
fixed to the ends of such boxes make them more easily portable.

Before going on to the question of gear there are a few extra
furnishings that might be mentioned, though necessarily these and
other things depend on the Troop's finances and abilities. A
knotting board with the Tenderfoot and other knots displayed at
various stages of their make-up is a useful exhibit for Scouts and
strangers. Model bridges, diagrams of bridges, outlines of trees,
collections of plaster casts, impressions of leaves, Scout posters
and pictures, samples of timber, mementoes of expeditions, maps
of the area of different scales, are all useful possessions. A tracking
box—any seedling box filled with sand—will enable the imprints
of track dies and casts to be made. A sand track outdoors, or even
indoors in a corner of the room as I have seen it will become a
treasured and much-used possession. In Canada use has been
made of a canvas box for tracking practices. The box, 10 feet by
12 feet, is made of rough timber 2 inches by 4 inches. The canvas
is tacked to the long sides and rolled up with them when the tray
is not in use. The ends are mortised for slipping into place when
the sides are unrolled and laid flat. The river sand is kept in bags
and fills the tray, when in use, to a depth of 3 inches. I have
detailed this tray specially as showing the possibilities of securing
the means of doing outdoor Scouting indoors when a certain amount
of ingenuity is exercised. An artificial camp fire is also a great
help in securing an outdoor atmosphere on occasions. There
should be no need to explain how such can be constructed. These
are only a few out of the many additions that a Troop can make
to its Headquarters if it has the opportunity.

### Gear

The question of equipment is somewhat different. Whatever
Headquarters the Troop uses it should possess a minimum of gear,
otherwise its Scouting will suffer. This gear should be overhauled
and put in order regularly every year, apart from the quarterly
check that is made by the Court of Honour. Gear should invariably

be placed in its proper place after every meeting, whether in Patrol boxes, Troop box, cupboards or the homes of Scouters and Scouts. If gear has to be brought to the Troop room every meeting, it is best to have one person responsible for it, or to place the responsibility on the Patrol Leaders for their special portions. Some gear is a necessity, and other gear is an extra, but it all depends upon the activities in which the Troop is indulging which is which.

There must be a good supply of real rope for knotting and lashing. A couple of knotting ropes and a long lashing to each Scout is not an extravagant amount for a normal Troop to possess. The ropes should be of differing sizes and kinds so that a certain amount of choice is involved if any rope work is to be done ; yarn or other material for whipping the end of a rope is also necessary. The cords that some Scouts carry on their belts are not a suitable substitute for knotting ropes.

Signalling flags, bandages, a few specimen splints will also be required. One set of bandages for each Patrol is sufficient, as Scarves are available if more are required by any practice. The splints need not be bought ; they are better made, and of different lengths and widths, so that again choice can be exercised.

Gear for games depends on the types of games played in the Troop. It is a good plan to have a special box for games gear, containing balls of different kinds, bean bags, sticks, grommets, and so on.

Camp gear so much depends on the nature of the Troop that it is impossible to detail any list of it. Tents, cooking pots, etc., should be carefully stored during the off season and periodically inspected and aired. Towards the end of the winter will come the time when everything connected with camp should be overhauled, repaired and brought up to date. This does not only apply to gear but to the knowledge and ability of the Scouts themselves.

Books should also be mentioned. Even if it is not possible for the Troop to have a small library of its own, it should possess a small number of books that can be loaned out to Patrol Leaders and Scouts. *Scouting for Boys*—more than one copy—*Letters to a Patrol Leader*, and certain of the " Gilcraft " books should invariably be included. After the Scouting section has been well founded, a hobbies and then a fiction section should be started. If the Troop has no permanent possession of its meeting-place, these books can be kept in the charge of an A.S.M. or P.L., who, as Troop Librarian, is responsible for them to the Court of Honour.

Before leaving the subject of Troop Headquarters there is just one more point to make. Whatever their nature may be, however insecure their tenure, whatever difficulties may be imposed, a real attempt must be made to secure something of a Scouty atmosphere. Even the opening of a window that has been closed all day may turn a parish hall into a Scout room, but more than that is usually required. As has been said, it is a challenge thrown out to the Scouters and Scouts to use their ingenuity and show that they can demonstrate themselves to be real Scouts by using the materials ready to hand and converting them to the best possible use.

## Tests

I have headed this chapter " annual repairs " of set purpose because it enables me to bring within its scope the question of the annual revision of Scout tests. I believe that every year, preferably in the autumn, the Troop should set about putting its house in order so far as its Scout knowledge is concerned. This necessitates going over old ground again, seeing that every member of the Troop knows his Tenderfoot tests, that every Second-class Scout knows his Second-class tests as well, that every First-class Scout still remembers his Second-class and his Tenderfoot as well as his First-class knowledge, that every King's Scout retains the knowledge that is implied by his qualifying badges. We owe this to the Troop and to Scouting, but also to the boys themselves to ensure that they are not masquerading.

It need not be a very lengthy business, nor need it be uninteresting. Patrol Leaders can be made responsible for seeing that the Tenderfoot and Second-class revision is carried out at Patrol meetings, or at Patrol time in Troop meetings. A few games and carefully devised competitions will soon let the Scouter see whether the knowledge is still retained. There are many varieties of games and practices that can be used for this purpose, and any idea of staleness will be removed by the variety introduced. Again, it is a matter of ingenuity and resourcefulness. For the first-class and further revision, a certain amount more in the way of work will be necessary, but that again can be incorporated in games and competitions, although there will be only a limited number of Scouts to deal with. Preferably a Saturday afternoon, or special time, should be set apart for this revisional practice and testing.

Some Scouters say that this repetition is unnecessary and that their Scouts grumble at it. It is not unnecessary, it is an essential part of the consolidation that has to be done before a further advance can be made. If the Scouts grumble about it, that is usually proof of the need for it. If there was no necessity for it, the time occupied in the revision will be infinitesimal. If it is rather a sweat to go over all these things again, they must have been forgotten.

What the Scoutmaster should do is to establish in the Court of Honour and consequently in the Troop a feeling that the honour of the Troop and of every member of it is at stake unless each one can prove every year that his knowledge of the stage he has attained in Scouting is up to date. Once that kind of a tradition has been established, the matter can safely be left to the Patrol Leaders and Scouts themselves. They will know when standards are dropping and will not hesitate to tell the Scoutmaster to be up and doing.

Repairs from time to time are always necessary if the house is to stand firm and safe against all kinds of weather.

## CHAPTER XVIII

### ENTERTAINING

THERE is a social side to every Troop that must not be neglected. The parties that it gives may differ considerably in their nature and their object, but some kind of entertainment must be given.

Mention has already been made of Parents' Socials and of Visitors' days in camp. These are occasions on which the Troop entertains its relations and friends at no cost to the latter. The Scouts are definitely the hosts of the grown-ups and should be expected to entertain them. A considerable amount of informality is advisable, so that the guests can join in the fun themselves. Games and contests can be arranged in which mothers and fathers can take part. Normally there should be no stage dressing ; the displays which the Scouts put up on these occasions should illustrate their normal work, so as to give parents an idea of what is being done. Each Patrol can be allotted a certain period of time and asked to draw up its own programme for the consideration of the Court of Honour which will draw up the final programme for the Troop as a whole.

On such occasions, whether indoor or outdoor, a short camp fire is a very useful ending. The Scouts and their guests can all be mingled together in the same circle, and a certain number of songs be sung in which all can take part. A five-minutes' yarn by the Scouter expressing the gratitude of the Troop for the help they have received from their friends will be deeply appreciated, and will do more good than any amount of appeals for help.

Troops can entertain, too, on a somewhat wider scale, again on a non-paying basis, by holding rallies in a hall or out of doors to which the public are asked by general or special invitation. The way this is done greatly depends on the locality in which the Troop is. A village Troop can hold a rally in the village hall or on the village green on its own, while town Troops can combine together, although this kind of entertaining will mostly be done by means of Association Rallies. Whatever the locality, however, it is important that Scouts should keep doing something to let the public know what Scouting is, what kind of things the Scouts do, and to prove to the people round about them that Scouting does enable boys to do things that they would not otherwise be able to do.

When rallies of any kind are held, those responsible—Scoutmaster, District Scoutmaster or Commissioner—should make certain that there is something doing all the time, and not only that, but that there is something doing in which the public can take an interest. Instead of one single activity taking place at one time, it is a good plan, if space is available, to take a page out of the old showman's book and to have several things going on at once. In the same way—indoors or outdoors—an arena is always better than a stage. For a rally to be spectacular there must be a mass display of the Scouts at the beginning and the end, and a breaking away into small gangs which maintain interest and activity during the interval. Quick, lively games ; light bridge building ; the erection of a signalling tower ; a short game of hand-ball ; tumbling ; erecting tents ; rope spinning ; displays of practical knotting ; a few minutes' silent drill by signals ; these are all proceedings which keep a rally alive. Every care should be taken to see that there are no delays between items, and that the arena is always occupied. A short rally with something going on all the time is much better, and more appreciated, than a long rally with interminable waits. One of the most spectacular finishes to a rally, especially if dusk is falling, and one very seldom seen, is combined parade firelighting more or less on the lines set out on pages 213–14 of *Scouting for Boys*.

There is always the possibility of holding larger and more spectacular rallies as a means of raising funds as well as of propaganda. The Jamboree Rallies are a case in point. Although we cannot achieve such numbers it is quite possible to achieve the same spirit and high degree of entertainment no matter how small our Troop or District may be. One important point to remember about these rallies and so on is that they are almost the only means we have of showing off Scouting ; they act as the show windows of the house and should illustrate some of the real work that is being done within the building. In our normal Scouting we don't want to show off too much ; the Scout is one who does his job without being seen, who prides himself on leaving no trace save a feeling of happiness. Mainly Scouting hopes to be judged by its results in the characters of the boys who are, and of the men who have been, Scouts. It is all the more necessary then that when Scouts appear in public they should represent Scouting in a fitting fashion. This does not only apply to rallies and displays, but to St. George's Day parades, Church parades, and various civic and national functions, as well as to the behaviour of Scouts and Scouters—in uniform or not—when in public.

A good deal more may be said on the subject of indoor entertainments. Many Scouters say that Troop entertainments are more bother than they are worth, that the monetary advantage obtained is not commensurate with the amount of time and trouble spent, that Scout work is neglected, that they upset the Troop and its programme. All this is quite true in certain cases, but there is no real necessity for it to be true.

An entertainment will be necessary in order to raise funds for

Troop Headquarters, for camping gear, for the ordinary expenses of the Troop. The question of money should, in the main, be a subsidiary consideration. Great care should of course be taken with the business side of the proceedings, but that side should be organised independently of the production side. There are two ways in which this can be done. The Troop itself can appoint a business sub-committee from amongst its own members which will go into the question of procuring a hall, printing and selling tickets, and all the other jobs so necessary to make the show a financial success. The other way, and personally I would prefer this, is to hand the whole of the business side over to the Group Committee, or a committee of parents. The reason I prefer the latter course is that it incorporates the grown-ups in the activities of the Troop and leaves the Troop itself to get on with the show. It can be argued that it is good business training to let the boys run the business side as well, but it is difficult for them to do both, and I doubt if they are old enough as a rule to undertake this responsibility. So far as the Scoutmaster himself is concerned there is no doubt that the latter will save him from an immense amount of worry and responsibility, which, after all, is a somewhat important consideration.

The criticisms of upsetting work, neglecting Scouting and so on are of course governed by the circumstances of the case. Generally speaking an indoor show can consist of three distinct things— Scouting activities, Concerts, Plays. These may be produced separately or two or more can be combined together in one entertainment. If Scout activities are to be part of the programme, it is quite obvious that Scouting will not be neglected entirely. If a concert is selected, practice at camp fires in camp or indoors during the year can be put to good effect. Of whatever nature the entertainment is it cannot be divorced from Scouting, since the Scout method and principles will be used in rehearsals, the team spirit will be exemplified, the necessity for true discipline and for the subordination of the individual to the good of the whole will be illustrated time and time again.

Even when preparations are being made for the entertainment, there is no necessity, and it would be a mistake, to concentrate on these at the expense of normal Troop work. It is only about a fortnight or so before the opening date that all the efforts of the Troop should be devoted to the show and nothing else. There is also the point that the boys' minds need to be focused from time to time on a positive objective, while the good effect of appearing and acting a part in public is an excellent corrective of self-consciousness.

I have been at some pains to go into these points in order to dismiss the suggestion that Troops which give entertainments are not Scout-like. We have to remember that all is grist to the Scout mill.

Whatever happens two points should stand out quite clearly in the minds of all taking part, no matter how small a part, in a Troop entertainment. First, they are going to entertain those people who are good enough to come and see their efforts, and repay them for both their money and the trouble they have taken. Second, they are going to show these people what Scouts can do even in things which they think are foreign to Scouting. As Scouts they are being trained to be better men than they would have been without Scouting, so, if they are performing in a play, they are going to jolly well show that as Scouts they can act ; if they are giving a concert, they are going to show—even if they have not got very much in the way of voices—that they can make a pleasing kind of noise when necessary and can all work in together as Scouts.

The whole Troop should remember that no matter what kind of a show they are putting up their reputation as Scouts and as a Troop is at stake. A first-class entertainment will leave a good impression on their audience and secure sympathy and support. A haphazard programme, badly put together and badly produced, will have a correspondingly bad effect and give the impression that Scouting as a whole is rather a poor sort of show.

I am constrained to quote from a Canadian work :

" More important still is the effect which a carelessly put-on entertainment may have upon the Scouts themselves, giving them the impression that it is easy to put on an entertainment to raise a little money and that the standard does not need to be very high. Boys of Scout age are likely to be quite careless anyway, and the Scout entertainment offers an opportunity of teaching them an excellent lesson in thoroughness. Take for example the work of the clowns. Boys do not realise always that it is harder to be a good clown than it is to take a ' straight ' part in a play. The boys playing the part of the clowns should be studying their end of it for weeks and even months ahead, the same as the rest of the Troop. The audience will expect clowns to be foolish, to be clever and funny, and at times to be surprisingly acrobatic. It frequently takes the best gymnast in the circus to play the part of the clown. In fact all the humorous situations in the play or entertainment require to be almost thoroughly and painstakingly learned. As another example, a boy is supposed to play the part of a tramp and starts in with the impression that all he has to do is to look shabby, dirty and lazy, forgetting that there must be the little pathetic, humorous or tragic touches to the tramp's life. His clothes need to be more than shabby and dirty. Their design should be carefully worked out so as to interest and amuse the audience."

It should not be necessary to point out that a good deal of Scout knowledge and training is required to put into effect even the two kinds of characters mentioned in the above quotation.

For indoor shows which include displays of Scout activities practically any of the items mentioned for outdoor rallies can be adapted, with the addition of such things as indoor games, contests of various kinds—quarter-staff, boxing, wrestling, judo, fire-by-friction contests, a potted day in camp, interspersed with some of those stunts that go down so well at camp fires by way of lighter relief. Care should be taken not to bore the audience with things they cannot understand, such as the signalling of long messages from one end of the room to another, and ambulance displays when all that can be seen is the bent backs of a number of boys.

The only thing that need be said about Scout concerts is that there should be something Scouty in them. If something of the camp-fire atmosphere is introduced, they are liable to go much better than if the Queen's Hall atmosphere is attempted. A good Scout chorus with everyone taking his part is enjoyed by the audience much more than a succession of solos. Humming and whistling choruses are very good accompaniments to any really good voices that the Troop may be fortunate enough to possess. A few instruments, even the humble mouth-organ, will add greatly to the effect. *The Scouter* contains from time to time various articles referring to indoor entertainments ; the number for November, 1929, for instance, contained several such, including the description of a good " stunt " orchestra and an excellent little practical article on stage lighting and effects.

The plays a Troop may attempt depend very much on the histrionic abilities of its members. It is better to aim high than to adopt what the boys themselves would call a " potty " kind of play, especially if it savours of the Eric type, where the bad boy of the village joins the local Scouts and eventually saves the squire's daughter. That sort of thing is neither fair nor on the squire nor on the audience. There is no necessity to confine one's choice to " Scout " plays, choice is only limited by the material available and the strength of the cast. One Troop has chosen the trial scene from *Saint Joan*, and more than justified its choice. The greatest difficulty the Scoutmaster will have at first will be the casting of the play chosen, but it will be found that in the average Troop there are two or three boys who are natural actors ; the leading parts can fall to them, and the rest be fitted in so as to suit their capabilities. It is not possible for all the Troop to have parts, but all should have some job in connection with the play allotted to them, such as scene shifter, property man, make-up artist, and the Troop should realise that each part is necessary and that the whole production is a matter of team work, whether on the stage or behind the scenes. There is an added value in entertainments in that they afford scope for the development of handicraft and handyman abilities on the part of the Scouts. So far as possible the scenery, stage properties and posters should be the work of the Scouts themselves, giving occupation to those boys who are no use as entertainers.

On the general question of entertainments only one more point need be mentioned. Let them be Scout shows from beginning to end. Let the boys take as great a part in them as possible. The Scouters should work in the background, except perhaps in some important play, where a definite example on the stage is a necessity. Above all, Scouters should refrain from inviting their outside friends to take a hand. If the Troop cannot put on a show off its own bat, it is much better for it to do its entertaining and money raising in some other way.

Finally, we should remember that we have opportunities through such entertainments as these to do good turns for other people. If we can give free entertainments to poor children, hospitals, old folks, especially at Christmas time, the prestige of Scouting will rise high in the neighbourhood.

### BOOKS.

*Play-Acting for Scouts and Others,* Monro. Brown, 2s. 6d.

*The Nelson Playbooks.* Nelson, 7d. each. (This series includes some of the best plays, not only in the English language but also translations from foreign tongues and classic dramas.)

*One-Act Plays of To-day,* Marriott. Harrap, 4 series, 3s. 6d. each.

*The British Drama League Journal,* supplied free to all Groups who are members of the British Drama League (Subscription £1 1s. a year), 8 Adelphi Terrace, London, W.C.2. (Membership also gives the privilege of obtaining advice and supplies of copies of Plays at very cheap rates.) A List of Scout Plays can be obtained from The Publisher, Scout Offices, 28 Maiden Lane, London, W.C.2.

## CHAPTER XIX

### THE GARDEN

*" The Glory of the Garden it abideth not in words."*

THE foundation stone of Scouting lies in the Scout Promise of Duty to God. Some small mention has already been made of that part of the Promise, but now it is necessary to go more fully into the question of the relationship of Scouting and Religion. By religion we mean belief in a personal God who is the controlling power of the universe and is entitled to worship and obedience. Those of us who are followers of the Christian religion hold the added belief that God has been manifested to the world in the person of His Son.

The Chief Scout did not shirk this important question ; his views on the subject of Duty to God will be found on pages 237–8 of *Scouting for Boys,* and further remarks on the subject of Religion on page 327. It is significant to notice the opening sentence on the last page : " An organisation of this kind would fail in its object if it did not bring its members to a knowledge of religion."

In the first place it is necessary for us to understand quite clearly the religious policy of the Scout Brotherhood. This policy is fully stated in Rule 3 of *Policy, Organisation and Rules*, in which the first clause is : " It is expected that every Scout shall belong to some religious denomination and attend its services." It will be realised that the religious policy of the Brotherhood is founded on a mutual respect between different forms of faith, *not* on the idea that forms of faith do not matter. In other words, as has been repeatedly expressed, our Movement is *inter*-denominational, not *un*-denominational. This point was further emphasised in a pronouncement made in March, 1928, to the following effect :

" Imperial Headquarters wish to remind Scouters that it is the first duty of a Scoutmaster to emphasise to his Scouts the first point of a Scout's Promise—that of duty to God. The manner in which this can best be done must depend largely on the nature and circumstances of the Troop.

" As regards combined Parades, Scouts' Owns, etc., it must be borne in mind that it is a rule of the Roman Catholic Church that its members cannot take part in any religious observances other than those of their own Church, and it is the duty of Scoutmasters scrupulously to respect that rule."

To fulfil its purpose Scouting must be wide enough to include men and women belonging to every school of religious thought, and it has been due to its expressed policy that Scouting has been able to achieve this and to hold together members of many different creeds. It is not just a question of easy tolerance, but of real respect, the remembrance that other people are entitled to their views.

In order to keep the position secure it is necessary that our religious policy should not only be clearly understood but also faithfully adhered to on the part of every Scouter.

Let me make it quite clear that Scouting makes no pretence to be a substitute for religion in any form or in any degree. Some Scouters have done harm by making such an assertion. A moment's thought will enable one to realise the impossibility of such a claim, and the disaster that would occur if it were seriously propounded. The love of the open-air can be no substitute for a real religion and belief in the power and goodness of God, although the open-air may be one of His gifts, given to us to use properly. On the other hand there is no doubting the fact that Scouting can be " a most excellent handmaid to all religions." That is a different matter entirely.

Every Scout promises to do his best to do his duty to God, to use aright the gifts that God has given to him, to follow his religion —the duty which binds him to God. There is an obligation on every Scouter which has been clearly expressed to teach the meaning of this promise to his Scouts.

Religion is divided into two parts—Belief and Worship : Conduct and Behaviour in life.

G

The teaching of Belief and Worship is the primary duty of the ministers of the denomination to which the individual Scout belongs. In Scout Groups controlled by a Church or Chapel, the Scouter's task is comparatively simple. He should practise the religious profession of the Group and encourage all his Scouts to do likewise. He should second the desires and activities of the Controlling Authority, not passively, but taking an active part in the development of the spiritual side of Scouting. In an Open Group the Scouter has a more difficult task, but by no means an insurmountable one, or one from which he need fly. First of all he should set an example himself by having a belief which he has thought out and can follow conscientiously. He should live that belief so that his Scouts realise what his attitude to religion is and that it is the guiding principle of his life, even though it is not, as it should not be, brought prominently to their notice. He should understand the religious policy of Scouting, in some such way as I have already tried to explain it. He should encourage the individual members of his Troop to attend the religious observances of their own denominations. He should show them that they can carry out their Duty to God and their Promise of doing good deeds by assisting in the activities of the denomination to which they belong, as singers, Sunday School teachers, and in all the other manifold duties which are connected with religion. The Scouter should also realise acutely that Scouting is definitely out for the all-round development of the boy—physical, mental and spiritual, and that none of these three should be neglected by him. The boy's moral qualities will be the outcome of this development.

Difficulties may arise in connection with the older Scouts of the Troop who have reached an age of question and criticism. Advice to them should mainly consist in an appeal to go very slowly and think very carefully. It would be wise to point out that it would be better to continue in that form of belief in which they have been brought up until they have thought out earnestly something which satisfies them completely. Naturally they should be advised to take their difficulties and questions to their own minister. If the Scouter himself takes some trouble to know that minister, he may be able to do a great deal with him for such a boy.

Another duty is placed on the Scouter to realise the obligations which the religion of each boy in his Troop places on him, and to see that each boy has the means of satisfying these obligations. It is especially necessary to see that this is so in camp. For example, there is the obligation of the Roman Catholic boy to hear Mass every Sunday, of many Anglicans to be present at the Eucharist, of Jews to respect Saturday as the Sabbath.

Right Conduct and Behaviour in life is that part of Religion in which every Scouter can take a real leading part. The Scout Law is the most effective aid we have in this connection, and it is supported by all Scout games and practices. The life and atmosphere of the Troop have their effect on the lives of the individual Scouts of the Troop.

Camp is one of the most glorious opportunities that the Scouter possesses of giving the real impetus to the boy that Scouting intends. It is not the clothing that makes the man ; it is not the tents and gadgets that make the camp. It is the essence of God in him that makes the man ; it is the opportunities for the development of that essence in Scouters and Scouts that make the camp. Dr. Morton expresses this idea in *Hike and Trek* :

" Last of all, reverence. This is the religious emotion *par excellence*. The boy finds it as he foregathers round the camp fire with the companions of his adventures, and for the closing act of the day—prayers. Here is the mood and the moment, more particularly so if the day has been marked by striking adventure or real danger. For then the boy feels in a very personal way that throughout it all he has been helped and sustained ; and the realisation of this transforms the emotion of awe into reverence. The day's experiences have not been wasted—admiration, awe, and reverence now blend together into religious sentiment. And how the setting of this final scene recapitulates these experiences and reinforces this sentiment ! . . . Under such conditions of contagious emotion a Patrol Leader recites the Scout Law and reads the prayer. Then comes the ' Good night, lads,' and the salute. *The boy has caught religion.* He simply could not help himself."

In Controlled Groups the use of prayers at meetings and in camp will be governed by the direction of the Controlling Authority. In Open Groups when prayers are used on such occasions—and this is very desirable—they should be of a very simple and entirely voluntary character. Suitable prayers for this and other purposes in Christian Troops will be found in *Prayers for Use in the Brotherhood of Scouts*.

There are two other rules connected with Religion. Rule 66 states that " Combined Church Parades of Groups of different denominations are not allowed without special permission from the Commissioner, and under no circumstances should *Scoutmasters* insist upon *Scouts* attending places of worship other than those of their own denomination."

This rule is the outcome of the realisation of the dangers that lie in wait for us if we fail to follow our religious policy faithfully. Controlled Troops or several Controlled Troops of the same denomination may, of course, hold Church Parades when they like and without permission. Other Church Parades should not be too frequent, and, when held, should be well done. The point of view of the boy himself has to be considered, and the Church Parade should be conducted in order to secure his spiritual welfare and to develop the spiritual side of Scouting. Any idea of holding a Church Parade for purposes of display or propaganda is contrary to good Scouting and repugnant to its ideals.

In Open Troops the greatest care must be taken to see that any

Church Parade is entirely voluntary, and no boy should be made to feel that he is acting as a bad Scout if he wishes to absent himself.

Combined Church Parades should take place at other times than those during which any Church or Chapel in the neighbourhood is holding services.

Rule 81 defines a Scouts' Own as " A gathering of Scouts for the worship of God and to promote fuller realisation of the Scout Law and Promise, but supplementary to, and not in substitution for, ordinary religious observances." The rule is quite clear. The holding of Scouts' Owns in a Troop depend entirely on local circumstances. In many Troops—Closed and Open—they have proved of enormous power for good in the co-operative development of the spiritual side of Scouting. The restrictions and courtesies to be observed apply with still more force to Scouts' Owns than to Church Parades, special care being taken to avoid any clashing with Sunday Schools. In addition every care must be taken to see that the Scouts actually take part, that the reading of the Scout Law and the lesson is in their hands, that they have a choice of hymns and prayers, that occasionally the talk is given by one of themselves. So far as is possible the arrangement of the Scouts' Own should be in the hands of the Court of Honour or of the Patrol Leaders. The more the Scouts themselves are associated with it, in its preparation and its practice, the better It should not last too long, and should differ—in its informality if in nothing else—from the boys' ordinary religious observances. Hymns should be a feature, should be virile and sung by all. Objective hymns of praise to God should ordinarily be selected. The talk should be short, practical and definite, and, if possible, couched in the form of a yarn. The whole gathering should be alive, happy and Scoutlike. A Scouts' Own in camp should be held preferably in the evening after the boys have had an opportunity and encouragement to attend their own religious services in the morning. The value of such a family meeting for prayer and praise has been expressed in this fashion : " The test of the worth of a Scouts' Own will be found in the faces of your Scouts and in their actions in camp, and in their remembrance afterwards. So it is that they are encouraged to live to be true Scouts now and evermore."

It is, I think, necessary to say something about the boy's point of view. His attitude towards religion and the deeper things of life is normally one of reverence and reticence. It is very necessary that this attitude should be understood and appreciated. The average boy will accept and welcome any efforts made for his moral and spiritual welfare without question and without remark so long as they are not pushed at him too forcibly or too frequently. If that happens there is a real danger of driving the boy in precisely the opposite direction. On the other hand, he will notice, and even remark on, the absence of any such endeavours on the Scoutmaster's side. A negative attitude towards the spiritual side of Scouting is no good, the boys will sense it, and may follow the example thus set, or may even resent the failing. We have led the Scout to believe through the Law and the Promise that there is a deeper and inner significance in Scouting, and we have to ensure that they are not disappointed in that belief. The other day there was an article in one of the evening papers by Dean Inge. "Religion," he wrote, "must be caught, not taught. A spiritually minded master is worth more than any divinity lessons. We must face the slight risk that a very dominating personality may force the boys too much into his own groove. A boy who shows signs of talking like a saint should be snubbed. Many boys will say what they think will please, not so much out of hypocrisy as from good manners. There is much unreality in emotional religious professions at all times of life."

We must not expect then to hear or see any expressed result of our endeavours ; rather should we look for it in the atmosphere of the Troop, in the lives of the boys, and in the various acts and good turns that they perform afterwards as the ordinary everyday matters of life. There is where both the result and our reward lie.

"So when your work is finished, you can wash your hands and pray
For the Glory of the Garden that it may not pass away !
*And the Glory of the Garden it shall never pass away !*
*Kipling.*

PAMPHLETS.

*A Lively Faith.* I.H.Q., free.
*The Two Ideals.* I.H.Q., free.

BOOKS.

*Hike and Trek,* Morton. Harrap, 3s. 6d.
*Prayers for Use in the Brotherhood of Scouts.* I.H.Q., 6d.

## CHAPTER XX

### THE OUT-OF-DOORS

HOWEVER good a home our house may be, we are not going to benefit much unless we get into the fresh air as often as we can. However good our Troop so far as the ethics and organisation of Scouting may be, it is not going to become a real Scout Troop unless it gets out into the open air and does its Scouting there as often as it possibly can.

It is well worth while reproducing the first three paragraphs of the Chief's explanation of Scouting in *Scouting for Boys.*

" By the term ' Scouting ' is meant the work and attributes of backwoodsmen, explorers and frontiersmen.

" In giving the elements of these to boys we supply a system of games and practices which meets their desires and instincts, and is at the same time educative.

" From the boys' point of view Scouting puts them into fraternity gangs, which is their natural organisation, whether for games, mischief, or loafing ; it gives them a smart dress and equipment ; it appeals to their imagination and romance ; and it engages them in an active, open-air life."

We must remember especially that last factor of an active, open-air life. Without that factor it is impossible for real Scouting to exist. We want to offer our Scouts the real bread of Scouting, not a mass of dough as yet unbaked ; it is the open air that is the Scout oven.

If you seek for further proof look at *Scouting for Boys* and see how many of its pages are devoted to indoor work and how many to outdoor work. Look at the titles of the *Camp Fire Yarns*. It is worth while reproducing these here :

Scouts' Work ; Summary of Scout's Course of Instruction ; Tests ; Patrol System ; Life in the Open ; Sea Scouts ; Signals and Commands ; Pioneering ; Camping ; Camp Cooking ; Observation of " Sign " ; Spooring ; Reading " Sign," or Deduction ; Stalking ; Animals ; Plants ; How to Grow Strong ; Health-giving Habits ; Prevention of Disease ; Chivalry to Others ; Self-Discipline ; Self-Improvement ; Be Prepared for Accidents ; Accidents and How to Deal with Them ; Helping Others ; Our Empire ; Citizenship ; United We Stand—Divided We Fall.

Five out of the eight chapters of the book deal wholly with out-of-door subjects and activities, and the open-air takes a prominent part in the other three as well.

Despite this clear lead that the Chief Scout has given, probably the majority of our Troops spend three times as much time indoors as they do out. Not very long ago a London District tried to draw up a formula so as to decide whether any Troop should be considered to be below Scout standard and need the combined help of the district. At first the formula drawn up was more or less to this effect : The Troop must hold two meetings a week, one of which must be out of doors ; the Patrol System and the Court of Honour must be in actual evidence ; the Troop must camp for at least seven days in the summer and two additional week-ends during the season. This would be a useful formula for any Troop to adopt in order to judge the standard of its Scouting. On the face of it it does not appear to ask for too much, but in actual fact the majority of Troops could not come up to the standard, even supposing the two meetings a week—as should be the case—include a Patrol as well as a Troop meeting. It is the open-air conditions which would bring most Troops below the standard.

It is an important point this, to which not only the Scouters of newly formed Troops, but also the Scouters of old-established Troops, need to direct their special attention. We must endeavour to the best of our ability to preserve the Out in Scouting.

It is not a question of fad or fetish, there is a definite need for open-air work if the boy's character is going to be formed in the best possible way. Altogether apart from any considerations of health and strength—and they bulk large ; altogether apart from any considerations of cleanliness and beauty—and they are of real importance in the formation of a boy's character—the Scout, as the Chief himself writes in *Scouting for Boys* : " can do very much more for himself than the ordinary mortal, who has never really learned to provide for his own wants. The man who has had to turn his hand to many things, as the Scout does in camp, finds that when he comes into civilisation he is more easily able to obtain employment, because he is ready to turn his hand to whatever kind of work may turn up." So there are real, solid, matter-of-fact considerations in favour of it all.

I have already said a certain amount in connection with this question in other chapters, but it is such an important one that it needs emphasis by repetition. We can, however, now go further and discuss ways and means of carrying our Scouting out of doors.

It is a good plan to establish a tradition in a Troop that whenever the weather is suitable meetings should be held out of doors, or, as an alternative in winter, that at least some portion of the meeting should be outside the Troop Headquarters.

The type of country or the nature of the town is an important consideration and an obvious governing factor, but not the final deciding factor. Too often, I am afraid, the line of least resistance is chosen, and little attempt is made to get over the difficulties. On the other hand I do know of many Troops, both in the country and in the towns, who have found a way round the difficulties that lie in the way of open-air Scouting, and who do the majority of their real Scout work out of doors.

The question is dealt with at some length in *Saturday Afternoon Scouting*, which will be found really useful, especially in town Troops, in connection with this subject.

The best thing for a Scouter to do at first is to go through *Scouting for Boys* with his Court of Honour, and discuss with them which of the many outdoor subjects mentioned therein it is possible for their Troop to take up. It will probably be found necessary to draw up separate lists for winter and summer. In making up these lists it is best to work on the principle that the good Scout Troop will introduce into its programme of training all the subjects mentioned in the book, and that every time one particular item is struck out it must be because the reasons for the Troop's inability to take it up are insurmountable. It is a positive attitude that should be adopted towards such subjects, not a negative one.

Leaving out the question of camping, which will be dealt with

separately, a few suggestions can be made as to the kind of thing
that can be listed in this way.  These suggestions do not exhaust
the possibilities, but are merely mentioned as types.  For instance,
in the winter and in the town it is possible to secure a great deal
of interesting training in such practices as Observation ;  Following
a Trail—using maize, etc., with which to lay the trail ; Disguises ;
Morgan's Game ;  Scout pace ;  Pathfinding ;  Treasure Hunts ;
Patrol Formations ;  Message Carrying and Intercepting ;  Star-
manship ;  and many others.

In the country similar practices can be adopted and there are
facilities also for the practice for other outdoor observation games,
such as Scout's Nose and Jack o' Lantern in an open field or
wood ;  Trails of various kinds in the daytime ;  Compass point-
to-points at night ;  Woodmanship ;  Pioneering ;  and so on.

In the summer possibilities in both town and country are greater,
because rapid motion of some kind or other is not so necessary.
All the practices already mentioned are possible and such things as
Practical Map-making ;  Map Reading ;  Nature Study ;  Tracking ;
Stalking ;  Scouting Games ;  Night Games ;  Exploring Expedi-
tions (see p. 61 of *Scouting for Boys*) can be added to the list.

I have made no mention of any of the Second-class or First-
class tests, but there is no time during the year which is unsuited
to their practice.

Outdoor occupations can be presented in such a way that it
would be stupid to divide an outdoor meeting into the twenty
minutes' sections which are regarded as desirable for an indoor
meeting.  The whole period available can be well spent on one
single activity.  It is the method employed that is all important.
The first materials that we collected for our Scout building—
practices, games and competitions—should be utilised.  See to it
that the Scouts are doing things, not just listening to a long and
dreary lecture, their attention being distracted by the much more
interesting things going on all round them.  Let them do things
and make mistakes, let them see the mistakes they have made,
then indicate a way in which these mistakes can be avoided.  Occasionally, and it is necessary that the Scouter should have real ability
and knowledge of one or two outdoor subjects, *show* how it can be
better done.  Let the demonstration be imitated, and return to
that particular practice another time to see if the lesson has been
learned.

As an illustration, let us say that a short and fairly simple trail
has been laid by one Scouter and checked by another.  The Scouts
proceed along it in Patrols, starting at different intervals of time.
They lose the trail, as not infrequently happens.  It is a mistake
to call them back all at once.  Let them realise for themselves that
they have lost the trail.  Let them search round a bit to recover it.
After that you can call them in and take them back to a spot 100
yards or so before they ran off, take up the trail again and go slowly
along it with them.  If they stick to the trail this time, point out

the " sign " that they missed originally, and let them study it from different angles. If they run off again, give the same demonstration, but with added emphasis. These are important methods to observe in our training.

Both in winter and summer it is possible to make use of Saturday, and possibly other, afternoons for Scout purposes. In the winter these could finish with a cup of cocoa and a sing-song in the Troop-room, in the summer an occasional camp fire makes a very good end.

It is on such afternoons that the Troop can indulge in what have now come to be known as " Wide Games." In the early days of Scouting it was the practice to devote a considerable amount of time to the preparation and carrying out of field-days. The military definition of such a term seems to be a stumbling block to some Scouters, but its figurative definition is more truly indicative of its Scout value—" a day of unusual importance or excitement " —while its literal sense is obviously a day spent in the open country. It is this kind of practice that is now indicated by the term Wide Game. There is need for a revival of activities in this direction both so far as the individual Troop is concerned and as regards practices for a number of Troops together.

*Scouting Games* contains a certain amount of useful suggestions in regard to such games, and the columns of *The Scouter* have proved still more useful. But practically any idea can be worked up so that it gives valuable practice in Scout qualities. Colonel Theodore Roosevelt, son of the famous United States President, tells the following yarn :

" My father was a sort of Scoutmaster to us, and one of our favourite games, which he encouraged us to play, was what we called ' Point to Point.' Father would pick out two points a good distance apart and tell us to make a bee line from one to the other without any deviation whatever. If we came to a river within a few feet of a bridge, we would have to swim across rather than use the bridge. Again, if a haystack happened to come into the direct line of our path, either we had to climb up over it, or, if we preferred, go through it ! The first one arriving at the distant point was considered the winner."

Some such a scheme has come into fairly wide use in recent years in what is known as a Patrol Obstacle Race, such as is described in Chapter XXI of *Scouting Out-of-Doors*.

A word might be said as to the general value of outdoor Scouting games in Scout training. Both the Scouter and the Scout can benefit from them. The Scouter has to use his brains and his knowledge of maps and of the country in order to draw up a suitable scheme. He should try and make it all work logically into some kind of a story. He can draw on legend and history for his ideas, and make use of the romantic appeal of Robin Hood, Pirates, Indians, Bandits, Smugglers. He can incorporate his rules into the descriptive matter of his story so that a certain part of the country becomes an impassable morass, a wood becomes a forest full of lurking evil, a passing shower which has dampened their bow strings makes it impossible for the archers on one side or other to do any killing. His story should be suited to the particular tract of country which he desires to work over. Particular care should be taken to avoid military tactics and the movement of the Troop in charge of the Scouter himself, every possible endeavour being made to strengthen the leadership of the Patrol Leaders. The Scouter, too, should obtain permission to make use of the ground, and see that that permission is not abused in any way.

The Scout is trained in stalking, in the use of cover, in observation, in initiative, in care of the country—crops, hedges, stock, plantations, etc.—in playing for his side and playing the game, in practically every Scout method and practice.

Such things as Rules of Capture should be carefully devised so as to avoid any promiscuous scrapping, and care should be taken to see that everyone has a part to play, and that capture does not necessarily put the captured out of action for the rest of the afternoon.

It is only possible to mention one or two games as samples, and to arrange them in some kind of a graded way. All of these named will be found in *Scouting Games :*

Stalking the Scouter ; Stalking and Reporting ; Lion Hunt ; Flag Raiding ; Bombing the Convoy ; Scout meets Scout ; Dispatch Running.

These are all games that can be played by one Troop. It will be found that *Scouting Games* contains separate chapters devoted to Scouting Games ; Stalking Games ; Tracking Games ; Cyclists' Games ; Town Games ; Night Games ; Winter Games ; and Seamanship Games. There is, therefore, no lack of material ready to the Scoutmaster's hand.

Great care should be exercised in regard to night games ; it is best for practice to take place in the daytime by the use of masks or smoked goggles. When actual practices take place at night they should be over a very restricted area and in fairly open country. If proper care is exercised and the training given progressively, there is scope for a great deal of interesting and useful night work.

There is only room to quote two paragraphs from *Scouting Out-of-Doors*—a book addressed primarily to the Scouts themselves, but of equal use to Scouters :

" The Scout study of nature involves all branches of the subject, the study of birds and animals, their cries, resorts and habits, the study of flowers and trees, their uses and abuses, the appreciation of beauty in nature and in art, and the realisation that God created it all for our benefit. The Scout practice of the open air includes among its branches pioneering, stalking and tracking, the joys of camping and hiking, fires and cooking, the romances of exploration and pathfinding, the fun of games, the happy companionship of the camp fire.

" If we neglect these, we miss the great appeal that Scouting makes to our imaginations, and we miss the opportunity of thinking out and doing things for ourselves."

BOOK

*Saturday Afternoon Scouting*, Stocks. Pearson, 2s.

## CHAPTER XXI

### SUMMER HOLIDAYS

EVERY family makes an endeavour to have one holiday at least every year ; some are not so fortunate as others, but there is no valid reason why every Scout Troop should not have a chance of camping every year. Camping is not so much governed by the question of finance as is so frequently imagined. Some of the poorest of our Troops, so far as cash is concerned, are amongst the best of our Troops from the point of view of camping. It is a question, as usual, of where there's a will there's a way.

It is fair to state that camping is an essential part of the training of the Scout. No boy who has not camped out in the open can hope to become a Scout in anything but name. There are naturally exceptions, as with every rule, but these exceptions are when circumstances are entirely beyond the control of the boy, as in the case of disabled Scouts, whose energy and spirit the normal boy would be hard put to it to beat.

Camping is such a vast subject that it is impossible for me to treat it in any kind of detail ; it is only possible to draw attention to one or two considerations in regard to it.

Camping is both the Scout's and the Scouter's opportunity. The Scout has an opportunity of enjoyment and of furthering his Scout training. The Scouter has a similar opportunity of enjoyment and of furthering his training, but, further than that, he has an opportunity of seeing the effect of his previous training of the boys, of putting into practice certain ideas and activities which cannot be done at home, and of studying the characters of each one of his Scouts to the full. Dr. Morton, who has already been mentioned, writes :

" Any reflecting person must be astonished at the neglect of the individual factor in modern education. In the realm of science we try to unravel the mysteries of electron and atom. We isolate the microbe. We dissect the infinitesimally small. We study through the telescope the stars in their courses and the beauties of planet and satellite. Yet in education we almost all ignore that unique and varied cosmos which constitutes the individual child.

" For heaven's sake let us study our boys through the micro-scopic opportunity of hike and camp, and we shall find them never monotonous, never stereotyped, but always INDIVIDUALS so dis-tinct that we are happy if we know well just a few of them."

I call to mind one particular Scoutmaster whom I have seen often in camp. He is never dashing about in a state of agitation and perspiration. Frequently he is in the midst of a little group who appear engrossed in their own conversation. Frequently he is seated complacently outside his little tent with a reflective pipe in his mouth. His voice is never raised in a strident yell so as to penetrate above the hum of the happy, busy Scout camp. His Troop most certainly does not suffer. The work of the camp is done, and well done too. Many and varied activities are indulged in, from the humble good turn to the accomplishment of severe feats of endurance on the part of the older Scouts.

Without any doubt that Scoutmaster is doing his complete duty by his Troop by allowing them to do the work for themselves, and, more than that, he knows every individual member of his Troop thoroughly.

Camping is an opportunity that only occurs for a few months in the year. Let us make the fullest use of it. Let it be the cul-minating point of our study of our Scouts' characters. We can achieve this by careful previous preparation, by training in camping over the winter months indoors, and over the summer months out of doors, and, more especially, by a proper delegation of duties to Patrol Leaders and others, more so than by a delegation of various duties to other Scouters. At the same time over-organisation should be avoided, and a regular amount of leisure and spare time allowed to the Scouts.

Preparations should not merely consist in the collection of the requisite amount of gear and grub, but in the training of the boys and the choice of occupations.

The actual choice of occupations depends almost entirely on the state of the Troop and on the locality in which the camp is pitched. In a sense the two determine each other, for the selec-tion of the site for the camp should be looked at from the point of view of the activities to be indulged in, and the activities depend on what stage in Scouting the Troop has reached. Many months ahead of the ordinary summer camp the Court of Honour should determine the particular subject or subjects round which the whole programme for the camp is to be built up. It is quite a good idea, for instance, to decide that pioneering, swimming, nature study, campcraft, tracking, woodcraft, the First-class Badge, or even the Second-class Badge should be the main theme for the year's camp.

Once a subject has been chosen, and a site determined on which will be favourable to the activities connected with that subject, there are still quite a number of preparations to be made. No step should be left untrod in order that when the Troop does arrive in camp it may be able to get on with the occupations it has chosen without delay and without wasting time in preliminaries that could have been dealt with beforehand.

There should obviously have been a considerable amount of training beforehand in connection with the art of camping itself. This training should start in the winter months with short instructional talks on various camping subjects, such as : Health in camp ; Camping kit ; Lay out of Patrol sites ; Gadgets ; Preparation of food ; Cooking. Demonstrations in connection with these various subjects should be given, and opportunity afforded for a certain amount of practice. Camp sites can be plotted out on a rough sketch map, or, better still, use can be made of models of tents and a model camp site laid out with them and other models. Even indoors it is possible to practice such things as tent-pitching, boards with hooks in them being used instead of tent pegs. This kind of practice can be carried a stage further by acting arrival in camp, pitching of a tent, despatch of the various Scouts in the Patrol to set about certain duties, unpacking of kit and gear, lay-out of kit inside the tent, making of beds, a pretence of going to bed (all lights being turned out), rouse, exercises, lay out of kit for inspection, and so on.

During the winter, too, gear can be collected and overhauled, so that all necessary preparations are made before the camping season starts. Small expeditions can be made on Saturday afternoons to accustom the Scouts to the pulling of a trek-cart or to walking with a pack on their backs, and fires can be lit and tea prepared out of doors.

If such steps as these are taken, camping will not be a closed and neglected book during two-thirds of the year, but will be constantly kept before the boys' eyes.

More intensive preparations for camp can start when the weather becomes more suitable. First of all care should be taken to see that training in camping is given to the Patrol Leaders and Seconds, especially the former. This should necessitate a short special camp for them only, over a week-end or otherwise. In fact the Instructional Patrol mentioned in Chapter XIV should be taken into camp with the Scoutmaster, as Patrol Leader, taking his full share of all the duties required of the Patrol. In a new Troop it will probably be necessary to have two or three of such instructional camps in order to give the real Patrol Leaders sufficient confidence to carry on with their own Patrols in the Troop camp. If a Scoutmaster feels dubious of his own knowledge of camping, he should set out to acquire some by attaching himself to a camp run under the supervision of an experienced Scouter.

It may also be possible to hold one or two short instructional camps for the Troop as a whole, or for a Patrol in it at a time. The week-ends afford opportunities for such practices, but care has to be exercised to see that such practices do not withdraw boys from the Sunday duties required of them by their parents and padres. It has to be remembered always that Scouting over

the week-ends must be distinctly subordinated to the boys' ordinary
religious observances. It is best to hold these camps within easy
distance of the boys' homes ; that is an easy matter in the country,
but by no means so easy in towns. I think, however, it should
be clearly understood by all Scouters that, if any objection is
offered to week-end camping after the subject has been discussed
and every endeavour made to meet divergent views, such camps
should not be held. It will, however, usually be possible to meet
the majority of objections likely to be raised, and to make arrangements so that the Church is not deprived of its choir and so on,
and at the same time to obtain practice in camping.

Obviously there are the various material preparations to make
in regard to a Troop camp, other than the question of activities,
but I do not propose to go into these here as they are fully set
out in the text-books mentioned at the end of this chapter.

There are, however, two other considerations which it would be
worth while to discuss. New Troops would be well advised not
to camp too far from home, and even to consider whether it would
not be advantageous to camp alongside another Troop or other
Troops. An increasing number of permanent camping grounds
are being obtained throughout the country, and these can become
excellent training grounds in camping for new, or even old-established, Troops. They are usually run under the supervision of
Scouters who know a good deal about Scouting and are in a position to give helpful advice. Occasionally, too, District camps are
held, and these are also a valuable means of training Troops in
good camping habits. It would be better for many Troops to
gather their experience in these ways, before venturing further
afield on their own. Experienced Troops can do a good turn to
new Troops by inviting the latter to camp alongside, but not with
them, so as to serve their camping apprenticeship. Both will
benefit thereby.

There is also a need for the early choice of the Troop's camp
site for the summer. This should be done, as has already been
mentioned, in consultation with the Court of Honour after consideration of many points of view, not the least of them being a
change of scene for the boys themselves. When the site has been
selected, and a visit paid to it, or, if that is impossible, a report
on it obtained from the *local* Scout authorities, then intensive
preparations can be started. These should include inter-Patrol
competitions for the lay-out of the site on paper, preparation of
definite programmes of activities, for both wet and fine weather,
the acquisition of information in regard to places of interest in
the neighbourhood, the posting of photographs and information
concerning the place on the Troop notice board, the issue of a
circular letter to parents, arrangements for transport and supply
of grub, and the sending of the necessary information to the Commissioner.

These various preparations, and others that there is no possibility of mentioning in so short a space, are very necessary to the success of your camp. You may consider that all this drudgery can hardly make your camp a success, but it all depends on the spirit in which it is attacked. You need have no doubt that there is much more joy in making a real success of the job on which you have set your mind than in just scraping through in what has come to be the proverbial British fashion. But these preparations are not solely concerned with camp alone, they have an influence on the training of the Scouts of your Troop, both from the point of view of their efficiency in Scouting and of their characters.

Camping is essential to Scouting, essential both to the boy's Scouting ability and to the development of his character. It needs thinking out, planning, rehearsing beforehand if its presentation is to meet with success.

In " Camp Fire Yarn No. 9," which contains almost all the essential information on the subject of camping, there are three paragraphs to which I should like to draw your attention :

" In Scouts' camps the tents are not pitched in lines and streets as in military camps, but are dotted about, fifty or a hundred yards apart or more, in a big circle round the Scoutmaster's tent, which, with the flag and camp fire, is generally in the centre. *This keeps each Patrol separate as a unit.*"

(The italics are mine.)

" Camping-out is the great point in ' Scouting ' which appeals to the boy, and is the opportunity in which to teach him self-reliance and resourcefulness, besides giving him health and development.

" Many parents who have never had experience of camp life themselves, look upon it with misgivings as possibly likely to be too rough and risky for their boys ; but when they see their lads return well set up and full of health and happiness outwardly, and morally improved in the points of practical manliness and comradeship they cannot fail to appreciate the good that comes from such an outing."

PAMPHLET.

*Cautionary Cuts for Careful Campers.* I.H.Q., free.

BOOKS.

*Notes on Camping.* Board of Education. H.M.S.O., is.
*The Boy Scout Camp Book,* Carrington. Pearson, is. 6d.
*Standing Camps,* Morgan. Pearson, 2s. 6d.

## CHAPTER XXII

### TOWN AND COUNTRY

THERE is a considerable amount of difference between houses built in a town and those built in a country, and it is somewhat the same with Scout Troops.  It is quite obvious that a Troop situated in a town has other difficulties to contend with than a Troop situated in the country, but the latter does not necessarily have the better of the bargain as so many people imagine.  On the whole it is best to start on the assumption that the activities and methods suggested in *Scouting for Boys* are applicable to both town and country.  Unless this attitude is adopted there is a tendency for the Scouter to tackle his job with a kind of urban or rural inferiority complex as the case may be.

I have no intention of telling you how you should do your Scouting in a town or in a village.  The book I have alluded to tells you that already.  It requires reading and adapting to your own particular circumstances.  Time has proved that it is so capable of adaptation if only thought is given to the process.

There is the inevitable tendency for a town Troop to confine its Scouting to a series of weekly meetings and a summer camp by the seaside in company with hosts of trippers.  I have already suggested various practices which will take the troop out of doors at all seasons of the year.  Clubroom Scouting has its uses, but more than that is required of us.

There are distinct advantages in being connected with a town Troop which are not always appreciated.  It is easier to secure a constant flow of recruits to the Troop ; it is easier, strange as it may seem, to obtain Scouters.  It is possible too for the Scouts themselves to see a great deal of other Scouts and to realise that Scouting is a real Brotherhood.  The Scouters in their turn can see a great deal of each other, exchange views and experiences and pick up ideas and advice from each other.  It is also possible for them to visit other Troops and see how things are done.

On the other hand, in the country, Troops are scattered over a wide area and are not in a position to see very much of each other. They become somewhat isolated, grow up apart from the wholesome influence of other Troops and sometimes find it difficult to realise that Scouting is a world-wide Brotherhood.  They have the great advantage, however, of having the country ready to hand and of being able to apply themselves to outdoor activities.  In order to do this it is frequently necessary for the Scouter to overcome the contempt that is bred by familiarity.  The majority of country boys seem to go about with their eyes blind to all that is going on around them in Nature, except in so far as Nature influences their own particular job.

This contrasts with the greatest difficulty that the town Troop has to contend against, the difficulty of working out of doors. Much depends upon circumstances, but pieces of waste ground and the town parks afford scope for a great deal of outdoor Scouting, and so do the streets themselves when judiciously used. The question of camping grounds raises still further difficulties, but a large number of urban districts are setting out to acquire permanent camping grounds in the surrounding country. This is a step which should not be delayed too long, either so far as District or single Troops are concerned.

To my mind the solution of the difficulties in both the cases of town and country lies in getting good Commissioners and strong Local Associations. Largely it is a matter of organisation from both the Scout and the business point of view, but it is essential that all the Scouters should make up their minds to pull their weight for the benefit of their neighbours.

A great deal can be done by associating town and country Groups together, not only through a Local Association which extends to both, but in the matter of definite personal alliances between the two Troops. Information and visits can be exchanged, the town Troop can benefit by being introduced to the study of Nature, helped out perhaps by specimens sent to it by the country Troop. The other can be helped by accounts of town doings sent to it from time to time, and even by the encouragement to take an interest in their own countryside.

It is as necessary for a village Troop to obtain the use of some kind of camping site near home as for the town Troop. The village community is so close knit together that it is a great relief for the boys to get even a few fields away and surrender themselves to the joys of Scouting in the knowledge that hedges and woods intervene between them and the village and so shut them off in a backwoods of their own.

So far as the formation of a village Troop is concerned, especially a village in the depths of the country, the Scouter will get little or no outside help, experts in different subjects are few and far between, and he will mostly have to rely on himself for everything. Too much emphasis, therefore, cannot be placed on the necessity of starting with a small number of boys ; to start with a lot spells disaster. A properly working Patrol System also becomes of increasing importance, and it is in this direction that the Scouter should throw his energies for the first few months. After a certain amount of progress has been obtained an opportunity may arise of meeting a neighbouring Troop at some half-way spot when a few games can be played. It is important early on that the village Scouts should see that there are other Scouts in existence ; the earlier this is done the better, as it will have an influence on their own efforts.

The number of boys of Scout age in a village is probably small, but the number can be easily ascertained and its fluctuations year

H

by year easily calculated. It is sometimes necessary to consider this point when starting a Troop, and when a Troop has been in existence for some time. Troops frequently die out in scattered districts for lack of numbers. Sometimes the solution lies in having different Patrols in different villages all attached to one Troop. Troop meetings can be held every fortnight or once a month, but weekly Patrol meetings will be held. The Scoutmaster would have a poor time if he had to attend each of these Patrol meetings, but there is no real necessity for this. If he visits one Patrol every week, he can exercise some kind of supervision and control, but he should encourage the Patrol Leaders to come and see him as often as possible. The suggestion has been made many times before that it is possible to run outlying village Troops with Scouters from a near-by town. The villages may lack suitable people to act as Scouters, but the small country town has a wider field of choice. This idea has been carried out in different parts of the country and found to be of great use. It gives definite scope for Scout work to Rover Scouts, whose activities may be limited by lack of Troops in the town itself.

Another way of encouraging village Troops is to take some pains to see that they have their fair share of district functions. Too often every Association and District activity is centred in the country town; all competitions and displays and rallies are held there. The difficulties of the village Troops are thereby increased. It is worth while considering whether some of these events, and Association meetings, cannot be held in different villages.

Some six years ago the Chief Scout dealt with village Troops in his Outlook in *The Scouter*, and I take the liberty of reproducing a considerable portion of his remarks, so as to add force to the inadequate help I myself have given in regard to this question:

" I have often heard it suggested that village Troops are more difficult to keep going than those in towns. In some respects no doubt this is so—especially if they adhere strictly to the same programme of work as do the town Troops.

" But living as I do in the country I find there are many possibilities lying open to village Troops which town Troops cannot command. And I believe that many of these possibilities will not only give healthful and educative activities to the boys, but will also be of real advantage to their villages.

" For instance, *Village Signs*. In a previous issue I gave a description of the village sign which we have put up in my own particular village as largely the work of the Boy Scouts and their supporters. This has had a very satisfactory success. It has taught the villagers, old and young, a lot of history of the place, and has drawn the attention of tourists and travellers to the interest that the place holds for them. It has established a certain civic pride in their village among the inhabitants, which goes to build up an *esprit de corps* and closer comradeship among them.

" Then there is *Nature observation*, keeping record of the early budding and blooming of trees and wild flowers, the migration of birds, the visits of otters, rats and foxes, etc.

" *The completion of local maps* with latest buildings, etc. The following up of *by-paths and rights-of-way* to see that they are still kept open to the public. The seeking out of *ancient remains,* of roadways, camps, wells, fossils, etc. The making of an exhibition, or, if possible, *a museum* of bygone implements, carvings, pictures, pillories and stocks, etc. The keeping up of old *local industries,* legends, dances, plays, songs, customs, and dishes or drinks. Tracing back the *family descent* of the older inhabitants. The care of the *War Memorial* and garden round it, etc. etc.

" Those and many other matters of local interest can be made objectives for the activity of the boys if the Scoutmaster suggests them (one only at a time, of course), attaching sufficient romance to them to bring about their enthusiastic pursuit. The results can be not only *good* but *very good.*

" There are tons of history lying buried in every village if only we would dig for it ; and there are antiquarian and field societies in every county only too ready to provide capable and enthusiastic helpers.

" A little over a century ago villages had their system of paying visits to each other, carrying their totem pole and headed by their band of instruments and singers. This made for a healthy spirit of neighbourliness and courtesy while inculcating a certain pride and *esprit de corps* in their own village. Something of this kind might well be revived by Scout Troops and would be no small boon to the country."

It does not seem to be lack of occupation that is required in village Troops, but imagination to see the activities that can be pursued and discrimination in their choice.

There is one additional point worth mentioning. The village is a small community, and because of this its attitude and habits can be the more easily influenced. It is difficult to imagine the possibility of a town Troop having an influence on its neighbourhood, though I could give more than one instance of this. A well run Scout Troop is, however, almost certain to have a considerable influence on the village in which it is situated. This conveys an added responsibility on the Scoutmaster, but it also gives him a real opportunity of marking the effect of the work that he is doing. His results are quicker and easier to see.

## CHAPTER XXIII

### THE SCOUT HOMESTEAD

So far we have concentrated our attention on the single building of the Scout Troop, but all the time that that building is in progress, and especially when it has been constructed, we should be conscious of, and pay attention to, the other buildings which, with ours, comprise the Homestead of the Scout Group.

It will be remembered that " a complete Scout Group consists of the following three sections—Cub Pack, Scout Troop and Rover Scout Crew—but may at any given time consist of one or more sections only." We should, however, do our best to ensure that the Scout Group is made complete, so that Scouting in our neighbourhood can become one complete whole, and can be of service to boys from the age of eight upwards.

Although there are these three distinct buildings in Scouting, they are grouped together into a common homestead so as to embrace the whole *Scout* family. That family has certain aims and ideals to which the members of it—of all ages—are striving. Some are in the nursery—although it would not be wise to tell a real Wolf Cub that ; some are in the schoolroom ; some have gone out to work and are beginning to make a way for themselves in the world. All, however, have the same family tradition and honour to uphold to the best of their ability.

In the last chapter of *Wolf Cubs*, Scouting has been likened to a road or journey, which goes on from age to age. The winding paths of Cubbing open into the pioneers' road through Scouting, and that road in its turn widens into the broad highways that run through life, and along which the Rover Scout can continue towards the ultimate goal of Scouting—good citizenship in this world and the next.

It is very necessary that all Scouters should realise this fact ; the journey is the same for the whole of Scouting, but the different sections of Scouting have attained to different stages on it.

It is because of the different stages, and the different ages of the boys themselves, that different programmes and methods are adopted. In the Wolf Cub Pack use is made of the imaginative outlook that boys of Cub age have on life and their own doings. Adventure, Romance, Yarns, Plays, Games and Work are all mixed together so as to secure the training of the young boy. The Chief Scout took the *Jungle Books* of Rudyard Kipling for his framework, and on that built a system which young boys could appreciate and employ—unconsciously—to secure their own well-being. In the Scout Troop use is made of the still more adventurous spirit of the older boy and the good qualities of past adventurers are pointed out to him, and he is asked to be up and doing so as to follow their example of courage, independence and self-reliance.

Inevitably this means that the Scout must learn to do things for himself so that he can gain strength and confidence. In the Rover Scout Crew the boy who is growing into a man is enabled to associate with others who have the same aims as himself and so obtain strength to develop himself as the happy, healthy, helpful citizen towards which his past training as a Cub and Scout has been directed. He is also given strength and help to make a successful career for himself. Rovers, according to the Chief Scout's own interpretation in *Rovering to Success*, " are a Brotherhood of the Open-Air and Service. They are Hikers on the Open Road and Campers of the Woods, able to shift for themselves, but equally able and ready to be of some service to others." Rovering " gives the older boy the means of remaining under helpful influences . . . provides Scouting for young men with its joys of Backwoodsmanship and Nature-Craft . . . ; helps young men . . . who desire it, to train for Scoutmasters or Instructors . . . gives young men the opportunity of doing useful service for others on a recognised footing." I have been at some pains to go back to the original for these definitions, for I feel that the passage of years has tended to obscure rather than clarify them, and that there is a real need for Scouters to realise what was intended by Rover Scouting.

In Scouting, then, we have a complete scheme for Citizenship built up in three parts, all of which are of equal importance to the boy at the differing ages of his life. It is the equality in them that has made me place them in three buildings bound together in the homestead, rather than place them on separate stories in the same building.

The aim of every Scouter should be to see that the boy receives the continuous training suited to his age and tastes, that that training leads him on in the same direction, and that he is encouraged to continue under its influence as he grows older.

It was in order to further this aim, and to achieve unity of purpose amongst the workers in the Scout Movement, that what is now known as the Group System was instituted some few years ago. The Group is a corporate whole with a Group Scoutmaster at its head. It is not necessary, although it is desirable, that the Group Scoutmaster should be confined to the duties indicated by that position ; it is also possible for him to hold a warrant as Scoutmaster, Cubmaster or Rover Scout Leader. That question depends on the man-power available. It is necessary that where the Group has more than one section, the Scouters of each section should agree as to the one Scouter who is to take control of the Group as a whole and should support him loyally.

The Group Scoutmaster is the head of the community, but not an autocratic head, because he has a Group Council composed of all the Scouters of the Group which meets frequently and informally in order to help him with the governance of the community. Together they discuss the policy of the community as a whole, any differences of opinion between various members of it, any activities which should be indulged in by one section of it, so that the other sections may fit in their scheme of training accordingly, individual members of the community who are becoming too old for one section and who should pass on to another, questions of financial and other administration. Through the Council they establish the closest and friendliest relationships between each other, obtain sympathy with each other's difficulties, and maintain an atmosphere of mutual helpfulness. In this way the common object for which they are all working becomes clearer and closer.

The Group Scoutmaster, as the head of the community, is the head, or chairman, of this Council and controls its deliberations and activities. He is the guardian of the Group as a whole and is responsible for its well-being to the Local Association and the District Commissioner, and through the Commissioner to the Chief Scout and his Council. He is the adviser and friend of all the other Scouters, and knows sufficient about their job to be in a position to help them, taking care not to usurp their functions or interfere unnecessarily. He sees that the whole Group is linked up together, that all the mechanical aids towards unity—such as the wearing of the same Group scarf—are in use, that the Going-up Ceremony between Pack and Troop and some similar ceremony between Troop and Crew are utilised and have an influence on all concerned, and that steps are taken by all the Scouters to secure co-operation in the working of their various sections.

The Scoutmaster of the Troop should have some knowledge of both Cubbing and Rovering, so that he can understand their connection with Scouting and can appreciate the differences of method and treatment that they demand. He should maintain a wide outlook on Scouting and not confine his thoughts entirely to that original part of it with which he is connected. In order to secure the right attitude he should take some pains to study the evolution of both Cubbing and Rovering and come to an appreciation of the fact that both are the logical and natural outcomes of the Chief Scout's original suggestions in regard to Scouting. The Scoutmaster should know the Cubs of the Pack, especially the older ones who are nearing Scout age. He should also keep in touch with his old Scouts who become Rover Scouts, maintain a friendly interest in them, and continue to encourage them to carry their Scout ideals out in their lives. In order to do this it is neither necessary nor advisable that he should become a Rover Scout himself. The master of a school does not have to become an Undergraduate in order to keep in touch with his old boys who have gone up to the University. If the Scoutmaster is also in charge of the Rover Section of the Group, there is still no further necessity for him to be one of them. There is something derogatory to Rover Scouts in the argument that to retain their confidence " the Scouter has to go down to their level and become one of them."

The Scoutmaster should also look in on the Pack from time to time, when welcomed by the Cubmaster, and so keep in touch with the doings of the Pack so that his Scouting can be different from it. He should be in constant communication with the Cub-master in regard to the boys who will shortly come up into the Troop, and should endeavour to know something of their characters before they do in order that he can place them under the Patrol Leader who will be most helpful, and himself know what kind of treatment he should give them when they come up into the Troop.

By the example he sets the Scoutmaster will encourage a friendly attitude on the part of his Scouts not only to the Cubs and Rover Scouts of their own Group but also to Cubs and Rover Scouts generally. By his example of friendliness with the other Scouters of the Group and of the District he will set an example of the real meaning of the Scout Brotherhood which will not fail to have its effect on the thoughts and actions of the Scouts of his Troop.

### BOOKS.

*The Wolf Cub's Handbook*, Baden-Powell. Pearson, 2s.
*Rovering to Success*, Baden-Powell. Jenkins, 2s. 6d.
*Wolf Cubs*, " Gilcraft." Pearson, 1s. 6d. and 2s. 6d.


## CHAPTER XXIV

### THE VIEW FROM THE WINDOWS

THE surroundings of one's home make a very great difference to one's life, the view one has from one's windows may be a cause for happiness or sorrow. Not only have we to exercise great care in the construction of our Scout Homestead, but we have to choose a site for it which, without being too conspicuous, will give it an outlook over all the surrounding country.

We Scouters have to think things out for ourselves, we have to satisfy ourselves in the first place that Scouting is something which is worth while, that it is something into which we can put our energies and abilities, that it is something into which we can put our hearts. If the heart is not there, it is but a poor job we will make of it, and it is more than a poor outlook for the unfortunate boys we are pretending to lead. Scouting is not a duty but a vocation, and we should sense something of the call before we embark upon it.

Having satisfied ourselves on these points, we can start to build in the knowledge that our own personal foundations are secure. In the process of building, however, we cannot afford to do without thought. It is the mortar which binds the bricks of our activities together, so that course is raised upon course with safety. Only by the continual application of that mortar, mixed as it must be with the real Scout Spirit, can the Scout building we are raising approach completion.

As we build we have to keep our eyes open all the time, in order that we can gain strength and knowledge from every encounter we make with other people—Scouters and otherwise. Some of us are in a position to be able to visit other Scout Groups, other Scout Districts, other Counties, even other Countries, and can pick up helpful information and advice as a result of all these contacts. Others of us have opportunities of attending Conferences or Training Courses, where various Scouting subjects are discussed, and where, as is frequently the case, the most helpful discussions may be those that take place behind the scenes in little informal groups.

We have all some means open to us of fitting ourselves for our Scout work. Some have more opportunities than others, but whatever our opportunities we will benefit very little unless we can keep an open mind. That is very easy to say, but very difficult of attainment. All of us are inclined to suffer to a greater or lesser degree by reason of our own preconceived ideas ; the less the reason for the idea, the more do we appear to stick to it. We are members of a Movement, we are helping our boys to fit themselves for life, to capture good citizenship, and so we ourselves must not stand still, we must be up and doing.

We are also members of a Brotherhood, and we must do our best to get all our Scouts to realise that Scouting is spread worldwide. The first of all the important events in a Scout's life is his Investiture. If he has been a Wolf Cub previous to this he will already have advanced a great way on the road to understanding. Right at the very beginning of his Scout journey we should be particularly careful to point out that he is entering a great Brotherhood of Youth, which spreads out from his own village or town throughout the whole Country, the whole British Empire and the whole World. As he journeys along he will remember that, and on that remembrance he will be able to build a wide outlook as little by little incidents happen which help to confirm his Scoutmaster's words.

We can introduce into the activities of the Troop studies and practices which help towards a complete realisation of the World-Wide Brotherhood of Scouts. Yarns of other parts of the world can be told, yarns of individual prowess as well as yarns of collective experiences. Men who have travelled far afield can be roped in to say something of their experiences. Correspondence can be exchanged with Scouts and Troops in other parts of the World, but it is advisable, if personal contacts have not already been made, to seek the advice of the Overseas or International Departments at Imperial Headquarters before embarking in any promiscuous correspondence. Our Troops can adopt Troops in other countries and keep in touch with them, exchange letters, reports, photographs, and even visits possibly. Members of our own Troops go abroad, and we should make every effort to keep in touch with them, and learn of their experiences.

These are only a few of the many means that we can adopt to arouse and maintain interest in Scouting in other parts of the world.   We do need to give our boys as wide an outlook as we can, and we do desire the World-Wide Brotherhood of Scouts to be a fact as well as a name.

It is not given to all of us to be able to attend the Scout Jamborees which are held in different countries, but whether we attend them or not we can all gather strength from them.

Let us build firm, let us build high, so that we can look abroad and see into the future that stretches down the years.   What does it hold for Scouting and for us ?   We cannot tell, but we can see visions, and we can strive to make our visions come true.

Speaking at the Massed Thanksgiving Service held during the World Jamboree at Arrowe Park on the 4th August, 1929, the anniversary of the outbreak of the Great War, His Grace the Archbishop of Canterbury said  :

" Twenty-one years ago a soldier dreamed a dream.   From his boyhood he had rejoiced in the life of a Scout.   In many adventures he had found that it quickened the mind and braced the will and made men good comrades.   His dream was that the spirit of the good Scout might make the boys of his own nation healthy, happy and healthful, and fit them for loyal service to their country and their God.

" To-day ' Behold this dreamer cometh,' and he comes not alone, but with a comradeship of nearly two million boys belonging to forty-two countries.   His dream has become one of the great realities of the world.   How deeply must his heart be moved as he remembers the little camp of a score of boys at Brownsea Island, where he first tried to make his dream come true, and contrasts it with this vast camp of fifty thousand, and thinks of his two million Scouts in every quarter of the globe.

" May I not dare say to him before you all, ' The Lord is with thee, thou mighty man of valour.'   I pray that God's blessing may be upon him and upon the world-wide company wherein his dream has been fulfilled."

The dream has become one of the great realities of the world. The mountain that loomed so far distant has been climbed and conquered to disclose a still higher mountain that calls for still greater achievement.

Listen to the clarion call of the Chief Scout's Farewell Bidding at the World Jamboree that marked the coming-of-age of Scouting :

To-day I send you out from Arrowe to all the world, bearing my symbol of Peace and Fellowship, each one of you my ambassador bearing my message of Love and Fellowship on the wings of Sacrifice and Service, to the ends of the Earth.   From now on the Scout symbol of Peace is the Golden Arrow.   Carry it fast and far, so that all men may know the Brotherhood of Man.

# INDEX

# USEFUL HANDBOOKS

## SPECIALLY PREPARED FOR BOY SCOUTS.

**STANDING CAMPS. A Manual of Camping for Scout Troops.**

By D. FRANCIS MORGAN. Fully illustrated. A new and up-to-date book covering all requirements for Campers. Paper Cover, price 2/6 net (postage 3d. extra). Cloth Boards, price 3/6 net (postage 4d. extra).

**PIONEERING AND MAP-MAKING.**

By C. REGINALD ENOCK. Second Edition, with Preface by the Chief Scout. Limp Cloth, price 1/6 net (post free 1/9).

"The scope of the book is a little wider than the title indicates, for besides the excellent rules and advice it gives for pioneering and map-making, it may be regarded as an elementary guide to mining, surveying, and rural economy generally."—*Scotsman.*

**ASTRONOMY.**

By T. W. CORBIN. The *Professor* of the "Scout." Author of "The How Does It Work of Electricity," "Modern Engines," etc. With many Diagrams and Illustrations. Price 1/6 net (post free 1/9).

**THE BOY SCOUT'S CAMP BOOK.**

By PHILIP CARRINGTON. Fully Illustrated. With Foreword by the Chief Scout. Paper Wrapper, price 1/6 net (post free 1/9).

**CAMP FIRE NATURE YARNS.**

By MARCUS WOODWARD. A collection of one minute yarns relating interesting happenings in animal and bird life suitable for telling round the camp fire. Paper Wrapper, price 1/6 net. Cloth Boards, price 2/6 net (postage 3d. extra).

**THE SCOUT AS HANDYMAN.**

This volume is very fully illustrated with diagrams and gives reliable information on the following subjects amongst others : Painting and White-washing, Repairing Gas Fittings, Ball Cocks, Tap-Washers, Sashlines, Window and Door Fastenings, Venetian Blinds, etc.

In Paper Wrapper, price 1/6 net (postage 3d.). Cloth Boards, 2/6 net (postage 4d.).

**THINGS ALL SCOUTS SHOULD KNOW.**

Over 300 illustrated paragraphs about the Army and Navy, Ships, Railways, Hobbies, and many other subjects. Cloth, price 2/6 net (postage 4d. extra). Paper Wrapper, price 1/6 net (postage 3d. extra).

**A FRIEND TO ANIMALS.**

By F. T. BARTON, M.R.C.V.S. A Handbook of Instruction for Scouts and Guides on the "Friend to Animals" and Horsemanship Badges. Pictorial Paper Wrapper, price 2/- net (postage 3d.).

**SIGNALLING FOR SCOUTS.**

By D. FRANCIS MORGAN and ERNEST SCOTT. (The Official Manual.) Crown 8vo. Paper Wrapper, price 1/6 net (post free 1/9).

**THE BOY'S BOOK OF SIGNS AND SYMBOLS.**

The Title of this book will make all Scouts anxious to possess a copy. Price 1/6 net (postage 3d. extra).

May be had of all Booksellers, or from

## A. F. SOWTER, Publisher, "THE SCOUT" OFFICES,

### 28 Maiden Lane, London, W.C. 2

Who will send a List of other Books for Scouts and Cubs on application.

Printed in the United States
94853LV00002B/286/A